O LORD, HOLD OUR HANDS

O LORD, HOLD OUR HANDS
How a Church Thrives
in a Multicultural World

The Story of Oakhurst Presbyterian Church

NIBS STROUPE AND CAROLINE LEACH

Westminster John Knox Press
LOUISVILLE • LONDON

Scripture quotations, unless otherwise indicated, are from the New Revised Standard Version of the Bible, copyright © 1989 by the Division of Christian Education of the National Council of the Churches of Christ in the U.S.A., and are used by permission.

Scripture quotations marked JB are from *The Jerusalem Bible,* copyright © 1966, 1967, 1968 by Darton, Longman & Todd, Ltd., and Doubleday & Co., Inc. Used by permission of the publishers.

Scripture quotations marked NEB are taken from *The New English Bible,* © The Delegates of the Oxford University Press and The Syndics of the Cambridge University Press, 1969, 1970. Used by permission.

Scripture quotations marked TEV are from the *Good News Bible—Old Testament:* Copyright © American Bible Society 1976; *New Testament:* Copyright © American Bible Society 1966, 1971, 1976.

Book design by Sharon Adams
Cover design by Lisa Buckley

On the cover: The banner is from Oakhurst Presbyterian Church and was designed by Virginia Gailey. Nancy Anne Dawe photographed the banner, and the cover illustration was digitally created from the photograph.

First edition
Published by Westminster John Knox Press
Louisville, Kentucky

This book is printed on acid-free paper that meets the American National Standards Institute Z39.48 standard. ♾

PRINTED IN THE UNITED STATES OF AMERICA

03 04 05 06 07 08 09 10 11 12 — 10 9 8 7 6 5 4 3 2

Library of Congress Cataloging-in-Publication Data

Stroupe, Nibs.

    O Lord, hold our hands : how a church thrives in a multicultural world : the story of Oakhurst Presbyterian Church / by Nibs Stroupe and Caroline Leach.— 1st ed.
      p. cm.
    Includes bibliographical references (p.).
    ISBN 0-664-22698-1
      1. Oakhurst Presbyterian Church (Decatur, Ga.) 2. Race relations—Religious aspects—Presbyterian Church. 3. Decatur (Ga.)—Church history—20th century. I. Leach, Caroline, 1947- II. Title.

BX8949.D43 S765 2003
285'.1758225—dc21

2002072079

Contents

Acknowledgments

This book is about God's movement in the life of Oakhurst Presbyterian Church, and without the dedication, energy, and sharing of the members and friends of Oakhurst, this work would obviously not be possible. We are grateful for all they have taught us and continue to teach us. We also give thanks to our family—our parents and our children—whose heritage and whose continuing love have deepened us and continue to make us human beings. We have a circle of friends who continue to sustain us and challenge us and give us hope. The Presbytery of Greater Atlanta has long been a partner in ministry with us, and without their spiritual and financial support, Oakhurst would not have survived. In particular, we want to thank David Dobson and Ella Brazley of Westminster John Knox Press for their faithful editing and Cheryl McKinzie and Pam Outerbridge for preparation of the manuscript. Special thanks go to Nancy Dawe whose photography of Oakhurst worship and work has shared with many others the light of Christ that sustains us.

Introduction

Filled with New Wine

I can hear music from the sidewalk, and it gets louder as we walk up the side of the old church building. People are clapping along with the upbeat gospel music, and I can almost feel the church swaying. It is chilly outside, but the small church sounds packed, and I know that it will be warm and cozy inside. We walk up the steps to the double wooden door, and there is a large "Oakhurst" banner hanging on the side of the church. The banner has, simply, an oak tree surrounded by a purple background. The usher greets us at the door and hands us a program. He smiles warmly and says, "Welcome back! We're glad you could make it." "Thank you," I say and walk slowly through the bright smiles. "You missed the best part," someone else says, and I smile embarrassingly because we are late, once again. "Don't worry, though, there is still some good music left." "Thanks," I say again. We find the only pew left with empty seats, which is all the way at the back of the church, seemingly reserved for latecomers.

Everyone is clapping their hands to "Put Your Trust in Jesus," and Joann Price, the choir director and soloist, is singing strong and loud. The air reverberates with her voice, and I can feel the music in my bones. The choir members sway back and forth with the beat, clapping their hands, and their multicolored shirts are bright and varied. The faces are as varied as the shirts, everything from pale pink to dark brown. I glance down at my program, and it says, "Sanctuary Mass Choir Rainbow Concert." It invites us to attend the "Gospel Fest 2000" in May, "Featuring the Hottest Gospel Choirs in Georgia." The choir sings proudly, and I can definitely tell that they are feelin' that music. Everyone claps at the end, and Joann stands up to give her thanks. She says, "Some folks say that white people have no rhythm, but we proved those folks wrong." Everyone laughs. Up above, at the back of the church, a brown Jesus looks over and stretches out His hands.

In 1995, Time Magazine *published an article about Oakhurst Presbyterian Church called "The Gospel of Diversity" (Farley, 1995). Why would such a church, a small Presbyterian church in the Decatur/Oakhurst suburb of Atlanta, attract national attention? Oakhurst Church has done what few other churches in the world can do. It has called people of different races, nationalities, and origins to worship together. Loosely classified as about "half white/half black," Oakhurst draws from all cultures to design its unique, and sometimes complicated, worship service. With a rich and extensive history, Oakhurst in the last three decades has been transformed. Surviving a crisis in the seventies, when the church almost shut down, Oakhurst has grown and prospered through the eighties and nineties, and now, in 2000, the church is once again facing change as the surrounding community makes another transition.*

—Jessica Page

*T*hese are words written by Jessica Page[1], a young African-American woman in the class of 2000 at Spelman College, who has since graduated and has now received her master's degree from Smith College in Massachusetts. She studied our congregation for her urban anthropology class, and her study was one of many that have been done of our life together at Oakhurst. Columbia Seminary, Candler Seminary at Emory, the Interdenominational Theological Center, and Union Seminary in Richmond are among the seminaries that have studied us. In addition to the *Time* article mentioned by Jessica Page, we have been featured on NBC Nightly News, National Public Radio, CNN News, and CBS Radio, as well as in *The Christian Science Monitor* and *Presbyterians Today*.[2] We are prominently profiled in two books: *Embracing Diversity* and *We Are the Church Together: Cultural Diversity in Congregational Life*.[3] We share this information not to boast about Oakhurst but to raise the same question that Jessica Page and many others have raised. In an age when megachurches are the hot items on the ecclesiastical scene, why all this notice for a 250-member congregation that has struggled for most of its recent history? The answer is that the power of God is seen and felt and believed in our life together. It is the same reason that those first Jewish folk were drawn to the church in its infancy stages. The second chapter of Acts tells us that people from all over the known world gathered in Jerusalem for Pentecost; that they were drawn to the tiny band of women and men who began to proclaim a vision of the power of God. It was and is a vision of God's new power that is breaking down the barriers of the world, undercutting the authority of the idols in our lives, and welcoming all people into new life in the Spirit.

To cross so many barriers and to do it for so long seems impossible in our culture. Indeed, those Pentecost pilgrims who first heard the disciples of Jesus speaking in many languages tended to dismiss them as being "filled with new wine" (Acts 2:13). It was seen as a view of reality that was distorted, a view that was unrealistic and naïve, irrelevant to the real world. It was dismissed as a drunken vision to be discounted. Although a growing number of people in our country are becoming more aware of how multicultural our nation is, there is still great resistance to crossing those cultural boundaries. Places of worship remain a stronghold of monocultural status for many reasons. Places of worship offer a sense of cultural rootedness, where people can relate to the mystery at the heart of their lives without worrying about how people from other cultures will react to their form of worship or their approach to God. In this sense, monocultural worship reinforces the humanity and culture of its congregants. For those who are oppressed in this society, monocultural worship is especially important. Worship becomes the central place where their humanity is affirmed, where they hear that their central definition is not that of the dominant culture but rather that of child of the God they worship, a definition that enables them to survive and even thrive in a hostile society.[4]

Those considered to be part of the dominant culture often choose monocultural worship for many of the same reasons, with one important exception. Places of worship that serve those considered "minorities" in this society have historically been open to people of any cultural background whereas white churches in this country have often refused to admit people of other cultures into their worship. In our history as a nation, it has only been in the last thirty years that most white churches, especially in the South, have allowed people from other cultures to worship with them. Such permission has also come with a cost—it often means that all who enter white churches as "minorities" must leave behind their cultural heritage and accept the mainline white model of worship.

In neither of these approaches is there interest in seeking to learn from other cultures. Most monocultural churches believe that such cultural mixing is not possible in any healthy way. Oakhurst and other multicultural churches stand as an alternative to these approaches. Like the first disciples, we too have become filled with new wine, with a vision of a reality that is as old as the gospel and as contemporary as today's headline news. In Acts 2, Peter responds to the skeptics by saying that these disciples are not drunk. He does not deny that they are filled with new wine, an image that Jesus himself used for his mission. Rather, Peter indicates that the new wine is not alcoholic spirits but the Holy Spirit. It is a vision that is difficult to imagine, difficult to build, difficult to maintain. Yet it is a compelling vision—as blaring as a siren in the city, as provocative as tongues of fire leaping around a room, and as inspired as disciples sharing their possessions. It is this promise and this struggle that has brought so many visitors and students to our doors and to our life together at Oakhurst. To move into multicultural ministry is to cross into a whole new dimension of reality, with all its promises and perils.

This book explores the journey of one congregation that is traveling through the land of multicultural ministry. While it is a story based in the history and experience of Oakhurst Presbyterian Church, we are not unique. There are multicultural ministries springing up almost everywhere, crossing all kinds of boundaries and barriers. We are sharing our story not because we are the prototype but rather because we have been doing it for thirty years now and because we have made as many mistakes as we have enjoyed successes. We want to share both our successes and our mistakes in order to help all of us see that this is a real flesh-and-blood, stumbling, bumbling, longing, hopeful, joyful journey. There are flashes of light, stinging moments of pain, deepening roots of abiding joy. In other words, it is a journey with the Holy Spirit, a journey in which we discover our true humanity and our true definitions as children of God, no matter how the world categorizes us. It is a journey in which we make the painful discovery of how much we have allowed the idols of the world to define us—a journey in which we are stunned to hear that God's grace and power are redeeming us and the world. And it is a discovery based not only in the proclamations of denominational bodies but in our everyday experience, as we come face-to-face with those whom the world tells us are our enemies.

We have made a startling discovery here at Oakhurst, a discovery that we did not seek—indeed, a discovery from which many of us flee. In a world that seems forever bound to the barriers and dividing walls of hostility, we have seen for ourselves, with our own eyes and ears and hearts, that God is breaking down those dividing walls. What we have seen on the other side of the walls are not the monsters that we had been taught to fear but the brothers and sisters for whom our hearts are longing. We offer our journey in the hope that you, too, have made or will make this same discovery. We offer our story so that you will learn from our mistakes and be inspired by the gifts of joy that the Spirit has shared with us here at Oakhurst. As we in the United States become more aware that we are multicultural, it is essential that our churches and other places of worship become aware of both the promises of life in the multicultural garden and the barriers to the growth of that garden.

We will look at the resources in our traditions, in ourselves, and in our life together. We will use many biblical references, not as proof texts but as evidence of a growing admiration for the Bible as a life-giving source for all of us and, most especially, for those of us in multicultural ministry. What we have discovered in our multicultural journey with the Bible is not a dead document with static rules for life but rather dynamic sacred texts that describe the human encounter with God, with all its accompanying joy and mystery and terror and resistance. Because of the different cultural backgrounds and experiences that our members bring to their encounters with the Bible and to our Bible studies, we have discovered a depth and richness to these sacred texts that has been all but lost in the battle over their authority in the various wings of the church. What we have found in the Bible is not a prescription for how we are to live but a description of how we are living—of how God is seeking to transform us—and an invitation into that dialogue, in our individual journeys, in our life together, and in the life of the world.

For instance, many of us have a greater appreciation for Paul's struggles in a multicultural setting than we previously had dared to consider from a monocultural background. In Paul's powerful paragraph that begins in 2 Cor. 5:16, where once we regarded Paul as a repressive man, afraid of women, afraid of sexuality, we now see him differently. Now we learn from his struggles; we see a person who had crossed cultural barriers and was welcoming the church into that kind of journey, a person trying to help steer the church through cultural land mines such as the leadership of women, the status of slaves, the status of gay and lesbian persons, and the requirement that everyone become Jewish in order to be a Christian. Though we do not always agree with his resolution of these issues, we do give thanks for his struggles and his leadership as he sought to guide people from many different cultures into unity in Jesus Christ.

"Multicultural, forward-thinking, biblically based, Jesus-centered." That's how we advertise ourselves. That is how we seek to live, though the struggles remain many and are sometimes difficult. We are committed to this vision of multicultural ministry—this is our story, this is our song.[5] We invite you to join in this story, to add your own verses, to find hope and challenge for your own stories and songs. While much of our denomination and our nation sees multicultural ministry as groaning in travail, we have discovered that it offers us a glimpse of the glorious freedom of the children of God. We came into it filled not with joy but with fear. We reluctantly said, "Yes," largely out of a desire to survive rather than as vibrant, excited pioneers. In the midst of our fears and our reluctance, we have been stunned to find that God has richly blessed us and deepened us.

This story is not about how great Oakhurst is. It is a story about how great God is. Left to our own imaginings, we would have folded and fled. The witness of our story, however, is that God has not and will not leave us to our imaginings. God is breaking in with a new vision and a new reality, widening our imaginations so that we can see visions and dream dreams that we previously thought were impossible. In this story, you will glimpse those visions as well as our daily reluctance to believe those visions. In this story, you will glimpse what we have found: that those very people and categories that we once feared are the vessels through which we have received God's blessings.

This is our story, and this is the promise that we have received, a promise so bold that it still often eludes us. God has broken down the dividing walls because we are meant to live in community, meant to join hands around the table in the household of God: "Join hands, disciples of the faith, whate'er your race may be; All children of the living God are surely kin to me."[6] Rather than being strangers and sojourners, we are now citizens of the household of God, to use Paul's image from the second chapter of Ephesians. We have discovered that God will not give up on us. In the midst of our resistance, in the midst of our limited vision, God has come to redeem us and set us on fire and fill us with new wine. This is our story.

Chapter One

We Have Known the Movement of the City

Our life has known the movement of the city: we were once all of one kind. Then our church became multiracial and felt small and insignificant. And our people were afraid, afraid of ourselves from different races, and afraid of ourselves from different cultures. The faithfulness of those who stayed and those who came gave us courage. By God's power we have been given grace through what we thought was our weakness. In the midst of our fears God has surprised us and blessed us. The diversity, which we feared, has empowered us to confront God's truth in the world. In Jesus Christ the dividing walls of hostility have been broken down. Though we are born into diverse earthly families, our life together at Oakhurst has led us to affirm that we are called to be one family through the life, death and resurrection of Jesus Christ.
—Oakhurst Presbyterian Church Mission Statement

*I*n the first chapter of Luke, the angel Gabriel appears to both Zechariah and Mary to bring them stunning news about the births of John and Jesus. In both of these epiphanies, Gabriel tells them, "Don't be afraid." When the angels appear to the shepherds in Luke 2 to tell them of the birth of Jesus, they begin their announcement with these words: "Don't be afraid." The Christmas story—and indeed the entire biblical witness—is aware of how powerful a force fear is in our lives. Much of our energy is used in seeking to calm the fear and anxiety that seems our constant companion, calming them through faith in God or through faith in lesser powers, sometimes using a combination of both.

The politics of the system of race and the fear that is generated by race has dominated our national life since the European beginnings of our nation. Neighborhoods continue to be determined by the fear in the hearts of white people about living in the presence of black people and Latino people. This fear was a powerful force in shaping the history of Oakhurst Church, as the quote from our mission statement[1] indicates. It is a fear that remains powerful though somewhat diminished.[2] In order to understand the context of the struggles of our church and many churches like us, we must set this fear and this movement in its historical context. A sign of progress in relation to the struggles over race is the difficulty younger adults have imagining the racial situation in the United States prior to 1950.

There was massive resistance by white people, especially those in the South, to the changes brought in with the civil rights movement and the U.S. Supreme Court.[3] Nowhere is this resistance seen more clearly than in George Corley Wallace's inaugural speech after he was elected Governor of Alabama in November 1962. On a cold day at Montgomery in January 1963, Wallace spoke for many white folks in the South:

> Today I have stood where Jefferson Davis stood and took an oath to my people. It is very appropriate then that from this Cradle of the Confederacy, this very heart of the great Anglo-Saxon Southland, that today we sound the drum for freedom. . . . Let us rise to the call of freedom-loving blood that is in us and send our answer to the tyranny that clanks its chains upon the South. In the name of the greatest people that ever trod this earth, I draw the line in the dust and toss the gauntlet before the feet of tyranny, and I say: segregation now, segregation tomorrow, segregation forever.[4]

A sign of progress in both rhetoric and reality is that it is difficult to imagine a governor of any state making such an address today. In 1964, there were one hundred black elected officials in the United States; in 1999, there were over ten thousand. The black consumer market in 1999 is estimated to be $350 billion.[5] Despite much progress, however, much remains to be done in regard to the system of race.[6] In the early 1960s, as the session of Oakhurst Presbyterian Church and many other sessions and governing boards of other churches began to wrestle with this issue, it was not clear what the outcome would be. We will take some time now to set the context in the former Presbyterian Church in the United States (PCUS), of which Oakhurst was a part, until reunion in 1983 brought the old southern and northern branches of Presbyterianism back together. In this context, we will see the fear and the struggle that was centered on race.

On May 17, 1954, the United States Supreme Court issued its unanimous opinion in *Brown v. Board of Education* that the "separate but equal" clause of its May 18, 1896 decision in *Plessy v. Ferguson* was invalid. It was a decision that had been decades in coming, and it had taken Chief Justice Earl Warren some months to build unanimity on the court over the decision.[7] With this decision and with the beginning of the Montgomery bus boycott on December 1, 1955, the movement for civil rights for black citizens began to come into public consciousness. At this time, the PCUS was the only major religious body to still have its ecclesiastical boundaries within the old Confederacy. The PCUS, or southern Presbyterian church as it was known, came into being in 1861, when most southern Presbyterian churches split off from the national body in order to support the new nation, the Confederate States of America. All of the commissioners to the General Assembly in Augusta, Georgia, were slaveholders. The PCUS would remain a separate body until reunion in 1983 in Atlanta with the United Presbyterian Church.

Although the Supreme Court's 1954 decision was directed at the entire country—indeed, the "Brown" in the title of the decision refers to a family suing the school board of Topeka, Kansas—the massive resistance to the decision came from the area where segregation had its strongest legal status, in the states of the old Confederacy. Though many national denominations were strong in the South, only one had its roots and its continuing existence there: the southern Presbyterians, of which Oakhurst Presbyterian Church was a part. The remaining years of the southern Presbyterian Church would be an agonizing battle over race and how to respond to the civil rights movement.

In a touch of irony, or providence, depending on one's view, the first religious body to hold its national assembly after the May 1954 Supreme Court decision was the PCUS, the Southern Presbyterians.[8] Meeting the next month for its 94th General Assembly, the PCUS passed a statement entitled "Statement to Southern Christians," in which it condemned legal segregation:

> That the General Assembly affirm that enforced segregation of the races is discrimination which is out of harmony with Christian theology and ethics and that the Church, in its relationship to cultural patterns, should lead rather than follow. . . .
>   That the sessions of local churches admit persons to membership and fellowship in the local church on the Scriptural basis of faith in the Lord Jesus Christ without reference to race. . . .[9]

These statements sent shock waves through the denomination. In his 1964 book on prophetic preaching in the South during these tumultuous years, Don Shriver sums it up best:

> For this reason alone, if for no other, southern Presbyterians' ears were stung rather sharply by a forthright pronouncement of their General Assembly: "Enforced segregation of the races is discrimination which is out of harmony with Christian theology and ethics." The impact of this single sentence upon the life of the denomination can never be measured, but it is

probable that no other sentence from a General Assembly pronouncement has in recent times received such wide quotation in southern Presbyterian pulpits.[10]

As Shriver and others have indicated, southern Presbyterians were ill prepared to receive this pronouncement because we had lived our lives with a sharp line drawn between our Christian faith and the policies of segregation. White Southerners were able to call ourselves Christians and at the same time, maintain segregation, by convincing ourselves that we could separate religion from politics. Southern Presbyterians led the way in this development; they were Calvinists who repudiated Calvin's call for transformation of the political sphere and instead adopted Luther's theory of the two kingdoms.[11] This ability to separate the two spheres came to be known as "the spirituality of the church," and it was a hallmark of white religious life in the South prior to the outbreak of the civil rights movement.[12]

At its center, the doctrine of "spirituality of the church" asserted that the purpose of the church was the salvation of individual souls rather than the salvation and transformation of secular society. This approach gave the theological framework for laying claim to being followers of Jesus while maintaining and benefiting from legalized segregation. One of the great ironies of this approach is that rather than separating faith from politics as it claimed to do, it formed a lasting bond between the two, allowing white Christians in the South to transform the God we meet in Jesus Christ to the God who approves of slavery. As we look back, the hypocrisy and convenience of this approach seem obvious. We must be careful, however, not to distance ourselves too much from this era and its way of marrying its faith with its political goals in such a subtle and powerful way. We do ourselves a disservice if we dismiss this system too easily and condemn it too harshly, thereby missing an opportunity to gain discernment into the ways that we weave faith with politics in our own time. Legalized segregation was maintained by the forces of the legal system and by "unofficial" violence, but the foundation for this system was built in the hearts and minds of people who were ordinary and decent. A monstrous system it was, but it was given legitimacy by loving and caring people.

Into this complexity came the whirlwind of the civil rights movement, and southern Presbyterians, as well as many other southern Christians, were drawn into the storm as the doctrine of the spirituality of the church began to collapse under the stress of the movement for justice. From its strong pronouncement in 1954, the PCUS General Assembly dealt almost annually with issues pertaining to race. In 1958, while declining to interfere with the right of a session (the local church's governing board) to determine the use of church property, it did condemn the use of such property for private schools whose sole reason for existence was to evade the Supreme Court decision of 1954.[13] At the same General Assembly, a list of guidelines was passed for helping congregations and other church bodies navigate as the body of Christ in such turbulent times. The list included these guidelines:

1. All people have been created in the image of God and are to be treated as such. Therefore, we should confront problems of race against the background of a world perspective.

2. Though differing in outward appearance men are essentially one; they have fundamentally the same needs, aspirations, hopes and fears.

3. It is God's will that the law of Christ, i.e., love or good will, be operative in all human relationships.

4. To do unto others as we would have them do unto us, we must seek sympathetically and imaginatively to understand their point of view, their needs, aspirations and fears; this is a rule for individuals, groups and nations.

5. The Christian conscience cannot rest content with any legal or compulsive arrangement that brands any people as inferior; which denies them the full right of citizenship on the ground of race, color or social status; or which prevents them from developing to the fullest possible extent the potentialities with which they, as individuals, have been endowed by the Creator.

6. The recent decision of the Supreme Court regarding segregation in the Public Schools must be recognized as the law of the land, and obeyed as such until and unless it is changed by legal and constitutional methods.

7. The public school system must be preserved and strengthened. To withhold the benefits of a public school education from any child; to prevent any community by punitive means from carrying out its educational responsibility is an unwise and dangerous expedient.

8. Freedom of speech must be preserved at all costs, without the danger of economic or political reprisal for those who express opinions contrary to our own.[14]

At its 1964 annual meeting, the General Assembly amended the denomination's *Book of Order* to state explicitly that no one could be excluded from worship because of racial classification, and this amendment was passed by the presbyteries in the next year.[15] At this same Assembly, a "Pastoral Letter on Race" was adopted that included these words:

This social revolution has been painful to the South and especially its churches. The peace that we associate with our faith has been shattered, the unity of congregations has been threatened, the purity of the gospel has been compromised. More often than not we have attempted to save our churches by ignoring the revolution, by maintaining that its issues were no concern of the church. In so doing, we departed from the historical and theological position of our church. In this departure we have not saved the church's peace, unity, and purity. There is no peace to this overburdened conscience we are carrying, and there is no peace when so many of our ministers have been forced out of their pulpits or shackled to them. There is no unity when the deepest division is between churches and churchmen of the two races with little attempt to communicate and be reconciled to each other. There is no purity when the churches propound no social ethic for their people but rather let them graft their views, picked up outside the context of faith, to Christian policy. The Church Universal may be invisible but it need not be inaudible. . . .

The Presbyterian Church U.S. through its local Sessions can be a saving factor in the life of every community, large or small, in our Southland. The social revolution is not over; there is yet time for every Elder, both ruling and teaching, to ponder the dignity of his office and the sacredness of his calling and apply himself, along with his colleagues in Christ, to the construction of a new society in which every person is accorded the quality of life due him as a child of God and as a citizen of this nation.[16]

The reaction on the local church level to these directives and communications of the PCUS General Assembly was decidedly mixed. Some congregations celebrated such a move toward justice. Some fiercely resisted, but most were in the middle, trying to puzzle their way through what seemed to be a labyrinth with no easy exit and seeking to steer a course rooted in basic Christian identity and duty—all the while recognizing the political realities of massive white denial and resistance, including in some cases that of their own pastors and members. A few examples will give us a bit of the flavor of the struggle. A session in Tuscaloosa, Alabama, passed a resolution in 1963 establishing a policy that would close its doors to black members. Later that year, it reversed itself by a slim majority and voted to open its doors. The decision caused considerable unrest among the congregation, but thanks to the leadership of its pastor, Will Ormond, and its session, the policy held. After Rev. Ormond preached about it in early 1964, one church member commented, "I think that was probably the best sermon you ever preached yesterday, but I couldn't hear it."[17]

At the other extreme were churches that refused to open their doors to worshipers who were a racial classification other than "white." One church in Mississippi acknowledged that its policy likely violated its Christian identity as it voted to exclude black people from worship: "Although we recognize that this is not what Jesus Christ would do, nevertheless. . . ."[18] Such resistance to welcoming all people to worship together as God's children provoked a crisis for the General Assembly leadership in relation to its annual meetings. The 1965 assembly was scheduled to be held at Second Presbyterian Church in Memphis, Tennessee, but that church had voted in 1957 for an exclusionary policy. The policy was tested by an integrated group in 1964, and Second refused to yield. The moderator of the assembly, Dr. Felix Gear, professor of Columbia Seminary and former pastor of Second Church, then moved the assembly to Montreat, North Carolina.[19]

It was in this ecclesiastical context that Oakhurst began to wrestle with its identity and policies. Oakhurst experienced the whirlwind of the civil rights movement not only from afar but in close proximity as well. African American people began to move into the Oakhurst neighborhood in the 1960s, and the white flight began. Oakhurst was faced not only with the struggle over civil rights as a national issue but as a local issue as well—black folk were moving next door. This neighborhood movement was not accidental. Oakhurst is on the southeast border of Atlanta, and the neighborhood movement was part of the movement of the city and the urban renewal of Atlanta. For years the city of Atlanta sought to control, mitigate, and move its black population.[20] Its white power structure came to see that having a biracial governing coalition would cause fewer problems than seeking to hold governing power in white hands only. It yielded this power only begrudgingly, however, as we can see in this letter from Atlanta Mayor William Hartsfield to white community leaders:

> Our Negro population is growing by leaps and bounds. They stay right in the city limits and grow by taking more white territory inside Atlanta. Outmigration is good, white homeowning citizens. With the federal government insisting on political recognition of Negroes in local affairs, the time is not far distant when they will become a political force in Atlanta if our white citizens are just going to move out and give it to them. This is not intended to stir race prejudice because all of us want to deal fairly with them; but do you want to hand them political control of Atlanta?[21]

Part of the development of Atlanta included the building of sports and entertainment complexes such as Fulton County Stadium (since torn down for a new stadium), the Omni (since torn down for a new arena), and the Civic Center (still being used). In all of these movements, black homes, businesses, churches, and schools were taken. For instance, almost one thousand black homes were lost in Buttermilk Bottom to make room for the Civic Center.[22] Where did all these people go? Many moved into the southeast Atlanta area including that part of Decatur known as Oakhurst. Thus, Oakhurst experienced the dramatic urban movement that continues to this very hour across the United States: white people fleeing from the presence of black people.

Oakhurst Presbyterian Church knew this movement of the city. The civil rights movement was no longer a theoretical issue—it was up close and personal. Oakhurst was a neighborhood church, and white flight threatened the existence of the church itself. It was a real threat—of the many white churches located in the neighborhood, only two survived with any continuity: Oakhurst Baptist and Oakhurst Presbyterian. Oakhurst Presbyterian began in September 1921 as a white, blue-collar church in Decatur, a small town whose western border touches Atlanta. From the Presbyterian point of view, it was a successful church—by its twenty-fifth anniversary in 1946, it had seven hundred white members. By 1960, it had reached almost nine hundred white members and was a prosperous middle-class church with a multitude of programs for its members, many of whom lived in the immediate neighborhood.

Life began changing, however, both nationally and locally. Black people were on the news and in the neighborhood. White flight began in earnest, and the church began to lose membership rapidly. By 1966, its membership had dropped to 702, and by 1970, to 336. By 1976, it was down to 115 members, and by 1982, to 80 members, a 90 percent drop over twenty years. In the midst of this drop, however, there was much activity and struggle. The first recorded comments came in the session minutes of November 1963. In response to one of the Sunday school recommendations that worshipers be seated without regard to race, the session noted this reply: "It has taken no action to prohibit the seating of anyone because of race or color."[23]

Oakhurst soon found itself in the middle of the civil rights movement as it was forced to decide who was a worshiper and who was a demonstrator:

> The Session restates its firm belief that demonstrators of either white or colored races have no Christian purpose in attending worship services of Oakhurst Church, and authorizes the Chief Usher to calmly and quietly state this position to the leader of any such delegation and to refuse to seat such persons. However, if physical belligerence is displayed, no physical contact or harsh words shall be resorted to by our officers or congregation. A note shall be handed the minister by the Chief Usher if such an occurrence takes place and the minister shall acquaint the congregation of the circumstances. However, recognizing that this is God's house, that we are in changing times, and, in the firm belief that the majority of the Oakhurst congregation does not wish to exclude sincere worshippers, we feel that "demonstrators" should be defined as follows:
>
> 1. Those persons arriving with placards either carried or in evidence.
> 2. Those persons of either colored, or white and colored races arriving and assembling in a group and requesting that they be seated.
> 3. Any persons displaying an obvious lack of a worshipful attitude.

All persons not defined as "demonstrators" by the Chief Usher shall be quietly seated, and welcomed as worshipers.[24]

Although it was seeking to determine what an "open" worship policy meant, it had already decided to continue its segregated policy on Vacation Bible School by voting to turn away black children and send them to the black Presbyterian church in Decatur:

> A motion was made and seconded that if any negro children came to the Vacation Bible School that they not be admitted. The motion was fully discussed by the Session at length. The question was called for and majority vote by the Session was, that if any negro children appear at the Vacation Bible School that they not be admitted. A motion adopted that if the negro children come, that they be instructed to go the Trinity Church in Decatur, Ga.[25]

This 1964 decision to refuse entrance to black children seems to have been a factor in the departure of its pastor, Reuben Allen, as indicated by one member: "Reuben couldn't live with the Session's decision to turn Blacks away from the church. His departure was a note of change in the world I hadn't realized needed changing."[26]

As these decisions demonstrate, Oakhurst Presbyterian Church did not leap for joy at the prospect of becoming a multicultural church. Indeed, it was dragged, kicking and screaming, into this new dimension of multicultural life. God did intend, however, for Oakhurst to shift, and God provided the pastoral leadership to make it possible to uproot the old and begin the new without killing the body. A succession of three pastors blessed Oakhurst with the fortitude and joy of moving into multicultural life: Jack Morris, Dr. Lawrence Bottoms, and Bruce Gannaway.

Jack and Joy Morris brought energy, vision, and determination to Oakhurst. Even more so, they brought a shift in approach. They would not wring their hands and fret about the changing neighborhood. Nor would they simply say, "We will not prohibit anyone from being seated in worship." Rather, they took a proactive stance: they would go out and recruit the new neighbors, regardless of their racial classification. They helped the church to move into this new community in two powerful directions: recruiting prospective members and starting programs to meet the needs of the community. In their seven years at Oakhurst, they did great work—the first black members were recruited; the first black elders and deacons were elected. Many community programs were started: Girls' Club, Boys' Club, Boy Scouts, tutoring. A black assistant pastor, Connell Osborne, was also hired on the staff.

Great progress was made but at a great cost. The membership continued to decline rapidly as it became clear that Oakhurst would not only allow black people to worship there but would also actively recruit them to become part of the church. When the new evangelism program began, two elders resigned immediately, and many families left. As the struggles continued internally in the church, a reaffirmation of this active recruiting policy was brought again before the session in July, 1968, and it passed by a ten to five vote.[27] All five dissenting elders left the church. In terms of members, Oakhurst seems to have failed during the tenure of Jack and Joy Morris. In the development of the people of God, however, Oakhurst was an astounding success under their leadership. They had done the most difficult work of all. They had shepherded the church from a group gripped by fear, foreboding, and flight to a group who began to see possibilities in the vision of a church that welcomed all people. They had helped Oakhurst cross the color line, and, in so doing, they laid the foundation for all that was to come.

The fruit of the work of Jack and Joy Morris would be demonstrated in the calling of the next pastor. Given the struggles that were enjoined under the Morris's leadership, the next person to be called in 1972 as pastor could not have been more surprising: Lawrence Bottoms, a black man who had played a prominent role in helping the PCUS deal with its struggles over race.[28] He was the first black pastor in the old Southern Presbyterian church to be called to a predominantly white church, a move so astonishing that it continues to be rare to this day. He was a veteran of having to negotiate as a black man through the labyrinth of white power, and he brought many gifts to Oakhurst. On reflection, two prominent gifts stand out. First, the calling of a black pastor sent a signal to everyone in the church and in the community: Oakhurst was serious about this—they were going to stay, and they were willing to experiment. Dr. Bottoms's willingness to come to Oakhurst was a sign that new methods and approaches would have to be tried in this strange land of multicultural ministry.

The second gift that Dr. Bottoms brought was the opportunity, for the first time, for many of the white members of Oakhurst to encounter a black man as peer, as equal, indeed as pastor. As we will see in chapter 3, the system of race exists so that this kind of encounter does not occur. The heart of racism is the assertion of white superiority over all others, and here in the flesh, and in their pastor, the white members of Oakhurst had to engage a startling contradiction to the idea that made them "white" in the first place. Because of his previous experience navigating through these volatile waters, Lawrence Bottoms brought a gracious invitation to all Oakhurst members to see themselves and to see others in a new light. Rather than through the dim and distorted light of racism, Dr. Bottoms invited folk to see through the powerful light of the beloved community of Jesus Christ, a community where all were invited to the table.

The daunting power of racism is that it can absorb many blows and still survive, and so it was with Oakhurst. Despite the great leadership of Lawrence Bottoms, and indeed because of it, the white membership of Oakhurst continued to shrink while the black membership grew slowly. Dr. Bottoms's energy was also drained away from Oakhurst by a great honor that came to him while he was pastor there—he was elected moderator of the General Assembly of the PCUS in 1974, the first and only black person ever to hold that position. It required that he represent the denomination in many capacities, and he was often away from Oakhurst during that year.

On the retirement of Lawrence Bottoms in 1975, the church faced a difficult situation. Its membership stood at 133, and its financial moorings were coming loose. Through the leadership of elders such as Jack Murrah, Nate Mosby, and Evelyn Green, as well as the Rev. Jim Andrews, Atlanta Presbytery was convinced to provide great financial support for the church. Indeed, without the financial and spiritual support of the presbytery, Oakhurst would not have survived. Presbytery's support enabled the church to call another pastor. This time they turned in 1977 to a white pastor who had been a missionary in Africa (Egypt, Ghana, Kenya, Malawi) for sixteen years: Bruce Gannaway and his wife, Ollie.

The Gannaways found at Oakhurst a white church with black members. Although Oakhurst had taken the formidable step of deciding to stay in the neighborhood and to provide ministry to community residents, its approach had been a decidedly "white" approach. Because of their experiences in other cultures, Bruce and Ollie Gannaway knew that the next step would be the introduction of other cultural experiences in worship and other parts of church life. These were introduced not as quaint, cultural outings that would appear annually but as practices that would begin to become part of the regular fabric of congregational life. Gospel music was introduced in worship, and African and African American stories began to show up regularly as sermon illustrations and object lessons in Sunday school. Worship began to shift from the quiet formality of regular Presbyterian worship to a bit of noise and more informality here and there. The community ministry and outreach begun by Jack and Joy Morris was continued and strengthened. Strong African American leadership was recruited from the community, and a children's breakfast program was begun on Sunday mornings. These changes, especially those in worship, were met with strong resistance. It was one thing to stay as an all-white church in a black neighborhood and gradually add some black members. It was quite another to begin to weave black life into worship styles and congregational structures.

The white resistance took many forms. The white choir director would sometimes deliberately sabotage the gospel music in Sunday worship.[29] Worship and membership figures continued to dwindle. The white membership was not yet ready to become a multicultural church. It was difficult enough to stay as a white church while adding black members, and movement away from the sacred tradition of white Presbyterianism seemed too much to contemplate or attempt. In their ministry at Oakhurst, however, Bruce and Ollie Gannaway had given the membership a glimpse into the future: if Oakhurst was going to survive, it would have to be as a multicultural church. The black members had some reason to hope and indeed to stay. The white members saw that there was a whole new world out there—some liked it; some ran from it, but the Gannaways had helped point Oakhurst to its home, and they had helped to build the foundation for that home.

In March 1982, the Gannaways decided to leave Oakhurst and return to the mission field. At this point the church found itself at a difficult crossroads. Membership was below one hundred, and the average attendance at worship was forty-two. Presbytery put increasing pressure on the dwindling congregation to close, sell the property, and reorganize or merge with another church. The vision that had been developed over fifteen years bore fruit however, and the membership refused to yield. They sustained the ministry as they had in other years when the church was without a pastor, and it cannot be overemphasized how important was the work and the vision of the membership of Oakhurst in getting the church ready to move towards a multicultural ministry. Pastoral leadership was vital and necessary, as we have seen, but the membership sustained the ministry. Indeed, they successfully lobbied the presbytery to support a full-time minister at Oakhurst one more time.

In February 1983, Nibs was called as pastor at Oakhurst. Though we previously had been the first clergy couple called to be pastors at a local church in the PCUS, we had just had our second child. Our daughter Susan was five months old when we came to Oakhurst, and Caroline wanted to stay home with her and our three-year-old son David. Caroline came as part-time associate pastor for evangelism at Oakhurst in the Fall of 1984.

Our journey at Oakhurst has been full of many learnings, many struggles, and many, many gifts. Our learnings began right away. When the chair of the pastor nominating committee called us to see if we were interested, we asked how many black folk were on the committee, and we were told that two of the five were black. This was a good sign to us that whites were not controlling all the power. One of the things that excited us about Oakhurst was that it already had a substantial number of black members—that difficult line had already been crossed. The committee came to Nashville to hear Nibs preach at Second Presbyterian Church, where he was interim pastor. Second was an all-white church at that time, and as Nibs gazed out at the congregation, his heart sank, for no black faces appeared that day. The two black people on the committee had not come, and as he preached his sermon, Nibs noted to himself that such lack of black participation was a bad sign. When Nibs ate lunch with the committee after the worship service, he noted the absence of the black members, and the committee chair replied that indeed one black member had been unable to come but the other one was present. Here Nibs discovered how much he had to learn about race and its ramifications and permutations—the black member was as light skinned as he was. It would be the first in a long series of blunders and learnings, a series that continues to this very day. It also taught us that a sense of humor was an essential ingredient to multicultural ministry.

When we went down to Decatur to look at the church building, we were in for a shock. It was large and old and musty and in need of repair, but what impressed us the most was the huge set of keys that was carried by the person giving us a tour of the building. It seemed as if every door to every room was locked and that we were in a fortress.

The white church had stayed in a black neighborhood and had even gained a substantial number of black members—the sheer tenacity of both the white and the black members had helped them to hold out against great odds. Yet the fortress mentality made it impossible for much growth to take place. The white folk who were left were not budging, and neither were the black folk. The locked doors in the building reflected this standoff. We determined that if we came to Oakhurst, we would need to break this stalemate and allow some fresh air to flow into the building and into the hearts of the members.

We came to Oakhurst for many reasons, but two were decisive. First, the color line had already been broken. There was not just token black membership at Oakhurst: almost one-third of the congregation was black. White folk had stayed, and black folk had come—an unusual setting no matter the time or place. In spite of the fortress mentality, we perceived genuine possibilities at Oakhurst. The foundations laid by the previous pastors were solid and hopeful. The second factor in our decision to come was the state of the congregation: they were desperate. They had worked so hard and so long to make this vision a possibility, and the response they got from the outside world was that they had failed. They needed to prove and to see for themselves that this multicultural vision could work, could give birth to a whole new way of being a church. And this desperation caught our attention because when people are moved by despair, they are more willing to experiment, to try new things. Thus we saw the possibility of space created for the Holy Spirit to open eyes and hearts and doors.

Little did we realize how much *our* eyes and hearts and doors would be opened. We had worked with black people on the job, in school, and in the justice movements in which we had been involved. We thought we knew black people and black culture. We had no idea how miniscule our knowledge was. It was a sign of our ignorance and, indeed, our arrogance as white people that we thought we knew so much when we actually knew so little. It would be one of many humbling lessons that we would learn at Oakhurst, and the best that we could do was to accept them and laugh at ourselves in the meantime.

We brought fear and excitement with us to Oakhurst. Being pastors there was not a total break with our past development, but our experience has been deeper and richer than we ever imagined. As a description of who we are and what we brought to Oakhurst, we will rely on the words of a book that described us in this way:

> Since Nibs' style of dress contrasts sharply with that of most black pastors, jokes are made about this as well. Nibs is a plain-looking man in his mid-forties with a twinkle in his eye. He is five feet four inches and trim, but one cannot imagine him enjoying jogging. He dresses as though clothes are far from his mind when he gets up in the morning, sometimes wearing a tie and sometimes not, sometimes slacks and sometimes jeans, sometimes shoes and sometimes sneakers. Clearly he marched in the 1960s and is still marching.
>
> Caroline, Nibs' spouse and Oakhurst's associate pastor, greets us also. Caroline is strikingly friendly in this setting. For the most part, I have seen and heard of Caroline before primarily in her capacity as minister of outreach: challenging the status quo at school board meetings; taking commissioners to task for feeble and discriminating housing policies; advocating for the community health center, drug addicted children, illiterate adults, low income parents. This morning she is not carrying those burdens. She seems excited and buoyant. She is delighted to meet my family and eager to make us comfortable.[30]

We have received many, many gifts as pastors of Oakhurst. If Caroline had to name one of the most significant gifts, it would be an abiding belief that God is working even in what appears to be impossible. One Sunday several years after we arrived, Caroline was experiencing an undeniable despair that Oakhurst would ever thrive. The Church had turned many a corner to survive, but would it always be so hard to see beyond all the work yet to be done?

One Sunday morning sitting in the pulpit before the congregation, waiting through the prelude, this sinking feeling was present deep in her soul. It was just after Easter, attendance was low, and the thoughts of being more than a "make do" church was weighing heavy on our hearts. Caroline looked up, trying once again to muster enthusiasm to lead worship to the faithful who had gathered. At that moment a young girl came skipping down the center aisle. Ashley was waving her arms as beautiful as any butterfly—a small girl with the gladness of a big heart. She was skipping to the music and, as a lovely butterfly, was happy to be alighting in a front row seat next to her beloved Grandmother!

At the greeting time Caroline gave Ashley a special hug because this beautiful, colorful butterfly of African descent had spoken the words of the psalmist—"I was glad when they said unto me, let us go to the house of the Lord!" The joy of that moment broke the despair of Caroline's heart. Caroline reaffirmed that Oakhurst knew the joy of the Lord and that God had sent Ashley to let us know of God's abiding love and presence each and every day, especially on Sundays!

For Nibs, the most significant gift would be a weaving of spirituality and justice in a healthy manner. As we will share in chapter 3, both of us grew up in white, Southern religious culture in which spirituality and justice were divorced from one another. Nibs grew up in a church in which the language of spirituality was central. He learned firsthand from the members of his church that God was at the center of his life, that God's love and grace were powerful and would bring him salvation. He also learned firsthand that while God was the center of his life, God was not the center of all of life—race was. The power of God stopped at the church door and in the heart of the individual. Spirituality and justice were separated in the white Southern religious experience because of slavery and segregation. How could white Southerners hold slaves and worship Jesus? They did so by privatizing spirituality and limiting it to the individual relationship with God. As we saw earlier in this chapter, this idea became known as "the spirituality of the church."

This split had a profound effect on Nibs's journey. As he began to discern that the white supremacy he had learned from people that he loved was not God's will, he began to move towards the justice part of that dichotomy and away from the spiritual side. He began to associate the language and concepts of spirituality with injustice and oppression, and the profound truths of Christian spirituality lost their meaning and power for him. The Oakhurst experience has helped him to regain some of that meaning and that power, as he has learned there that the divorce between justice and spirituality that he received from his white heritage is a false dichotomy, a way of interpreting the world and God's will that enabled white people to retain their power.

Our experience at Oakhurst has been one reflected in the words from the mission statement that began this chapter: "By God's power we have been given grace through what we thought was our weakness. In the midst of our fears, God has surprised us and blessed us." As will be evident in this book, our journey together at Oakhurst has been one where we have often asked God to guide our feet. As the African American spiritual emphasizes, we need God's guidance because the obstacles are great, and the storms are many— obstacles and storms from the world and from inside ourselves. We ask God to guide us and sustain us, as did those people from whose hearts and whose lips the spiritual first emerged: O Lord, hold our hands.[31]

Oakhurst has been a church that has known the movement of the city. We have gone from a church whose racial makeup was as important to its identity as was the gospel to a church seeking to live out its calling as the body of Christ, still limited in our vision by the powers of the world, still struggling to follow the guidance of the Spirit. We have been gifted with many visionaries and pioneers, and we are thus surrounded by a great cloud of witnesses. Our goal is to create space for the Spirit in our hearts and in our life together, where there can be genuine dialogue, mutual understanding, and acceptance of one another, sending us out into the world to proclaim a whole new reality centered in God's revelation to us in Jesus Christ.

Chapter Two

Oakhurst Is a Remarkable Place: Different Cultures Really *Can* Come Together

> *Oakhurst Presbyterian Church is unremarkable on the outside, but the congregation inside is quite remarkable. . . . People from the most divergent backgrounds—middle-class professionals, blue-collar and pink-collar workers, welfare recipients, old, young, and very young, black, white, Asian, gay and straight. All seem to feel comfortable there, and speak their minds.*
> —Ted Clark, NPR, "All Things Considered"

*T*here is something about the Oakhurst experience. Jessica Page expressed it in the opening words of the Introduction. Ted Clark of National Public Radio was touched by it as indicated in the quote above.[1] In 2001 our church was named one of three hundred excellent Protestant congregations in the country in a study financed by the Lilly Foundation. Ed Albright, the executive presbyter of Greater Atlanta Presbytery, wrote a letter congratulating us on this achievement and also expressing his surprise at how often Oakhurst appeared in a fund-raising video for presbytery:

> As we all know, Oakhurst is highly featured in the new Capital Funds Campaign video. I can't help but think that the technicians who filmed at your church got taken up in the ethos of the Oakhurst Church and, therefore, produced so much footage that could not be omitted from this video.[2]

Joan Salmon Campbell preached at our church during her year as moderator of our denomination's General Assembly. She, too, was struck by the Oakhurst experience: "It has been a long, long time since I have worshiped in a congregation quite like this one. I celebrate who you are. I dare say you are one of the best kept secrets in the entire denomination, for rarely do I see a congregation so diverse, as you represent so many different kinds of people.[3]

What happened? What enabled this congregation to shift from a huge one dominated by race to a smaller one that became so striking and so remarkable that it often stuns those who enter its worship? We will seek to unfold this story in the rest of this book. Indeed, we have already begun to open its doors in the first chapter. Oakhurst was not transformed by us. Oakhurst was transformed through a long journey of crisis and travail, of joy and sorrow, of failed experiments and surprising successes. Oakhurst was transformed through the power of God acting in the lives of those who sought to be faithful. We cannot overemphasize that this book is not about how great Oakhurst is. It is about how great God is. It is about the resources that God makes available to us in God's great mercy and calling. It is about God's using fragile and flawed vessels to proclaim the vision of the welcoming and inclusive beloved community.

The leadership and membership of Oakhurst are not people who are fiery visionaries, wrestling with God and with humanity to build a brand-new world. The congregation at Oakhurst is much more like Peter and Mary Magdalene than we are like Jesus. Like Peter, we believe we know the answers and are often humbled in discovering how little we do know. Like Peter, we often weep when we discover how much the principalities and powers have captured our hearts and have caused us to lead lives that deny we even know Jesus. Like Mary Magdalene, we are so trapped by the idols of the world that we seem demon possessed. Like Mary Magdalene, we are often unable to recognize the risen Jesus when he stands right in front of us. Yet like Peter and Mary Magdalene, we hunger for the God who is revealed in Jesus Christ. So we come, hungry and longing, looking for the living water, seeking to be faithful, telling Jesus that we believe but needing help with our unbelief. We step out onto the water in faith as Peter did, and we take a few steps, but then the winds of the world begin to swirl around us. Fear grips our hearts, and we sink, crying out, "Save us, Jesus!" We come to the powers of death as Mary came to the tomb of Jesus, loyal to Jesus but unable to believe that death can be conquered. As Mary gained a glimpse of the risen Jesus, so have we, and we seek to proclaim as she did, "We have seen the Lord!"[4]

We at Oakhurst continue to have struggles and difficulties, but we have also begun to believe in and even to seek to live in the new reality of the God movement. Our journey continues through the faithfulness of God and the faith of our people. Stumbling and bumbling, maddened at times, saddened at times, discouraged and yet faithful, having moments of recognizing the risen Jesus, we continue to seek to worship and to follow the living God that we have seen in Jesus Christ and that we have experienced in our life together. In our journey as a congregation, we have been guided by three principles:

1. God is the center of life and our lives.
2. God likes diversity and offers it as a gift to us.
3. We continue to have trouble believing and accepting principles 1 and 2.

God Is the Center

At Oakhurst, we seek to acknowledge and to live in the reality that God is at the center of life and at the center of our lives. This proclamation puts God over and under all other categories of life. This proclamation emphasizes that God has priority over all the other categories that seek to define us: race, gender, money, sexual orientation, and nationality, to name a few. W. H. Auden wrote a poem about love which began: "He was my North, my South, my East and West."[5]

At Oakhurst, we have adapted that poem, and we seek to lift up that same sense of love and centeredness in God's relationship to us and our relationship to God: God is our east, our west, our north, our south. God is our compass when we lose our direction and can't tell east from west or north from south. When our Sanctuary Mass Choir sings from the African American tradition, "God is the meaning and the source of my life," it is a powerful affirmation that God is at the center of our lives.

Who is this God at the center of our lives? It is the God revealed to us in Jesus Christ, the God whose work is to make us know how much we are loved and desired, the God whose love is so deep and so vulnerable that God gives up God's precious child for us, the God whose purposeful activity seeks to bring us all to the time when every knee shall bow and every tongue confess. We affirm God's love for us as seen in the life, death, and resurrection of Jesus Christ. God loves us—each of us and all of us. We lift up the good news that God's love is deep and broad and is intended for us all. We seek to proclaim that there is no place inside or outside ourselves where we can go without God being with us. As the psalmist says in Psalm 139—"Where can I flee from your presence?" God is the center of our lives—we emphasize this again and again. We are given life by God; we are given meaning by God; we belong to God.

This is astonishingly good news! No matter what the world tells us; no matter what we tell ourselves; no matter what the world does to us, we belong to God. It is this kind of faith that enabled some white people to stay at Oakhurst when things seemed to be collapsing. When it began to be revealed that race was more important than the gospel, some white folk sought to live out of a different reality, a biblical reality that told them that nothing was more important than God. This faith enabled the small group of white people at Oakhurst to stay as the white congregation dwindled and as black people came to worship. As white friends departed and few white folk emerged to replace them, this group felt discouragement and a deep sense of loss, but their faith that God was calling them into this ministry enabled them to persevere.

We belong to God—we are God's children, daughters and sons claimed by God. It was this kind of faith that enabled black people to endure the horrors of slavery and the degradation of segregation. It was this kind of faith that enabled black people to dare to come to Oakhurst and to stay here, even as they received all kinds of signals that their blackness and their culture were not initially welcome. Their music was belittled, and their perceptions were discounted and even denied. Their souls were often hungry, but this sense of being defined by God and called by God enabled them to hold fast at Oakhurst.

African Americans brought this concept of a transforming God to Oakhurst. The Presbyterian God has often been a stern God, a God who almost delights in crushing sinners, a God who will get us unless we do right. Although one of our founders, John Calvin, indicated that our chief purpose is to glorify God and enjoy God forever, Presbyterians are not often accused of enjoying God in worship in a glorious fashion.[6] Indeed, our nickname is the "frozen chosen." The African American tradition brings a sense of celebration to American religious life, a sense of affirming in body and mind that God is the center of our lives, that God has claimed us as daughters and sons, that the presence of God can be enjoyed. It is a gift that African Americans also brought to Oakhurst.

For white Presbyterians and for most other white denominations, God is oppressive and repressive, a deity who is terrible and angry. African Americans understand this wrathful side of God, seen in the dead first-born children of Egypt, seen in the exile of Israel, seen in the 600,000 lives lost in the Civil War. Yet they also bring another side of God to the religious table—God as life-giving and life-sustaining. When the categories of the world tell us that we are nobody because we are poor or are the wrong race or gender, God tells us that we are a precious child of the God of all that is. When the categories of the world tell us that we are somebody because we are comfortable or because we have power, God turns over the furniture in our hearts, helping us to find our true definition as children of God. God wants to say, "Yes" to us and have us say, "Yes" to God. Sometimes that movement comes as God reaches down to cradle us in our pain, or as God twirls us to help us dance our blues away, or as God challenges us in our apathy and injustice and shatters our categories.

Thus the first principle of multicultural life at Oakhurst is that God is the center of our lives, and it is great news! Yet we do not always receive it as great news. The idea that God is at the center of life, that we are defined by God, is often heard as disturbing and bad news. When it is revealed to us how much we have allowed the powers of the world to define us, it is often too much to hear, and we flee for our lives. When it is revealed how much we have allowed the idea of white supremacy to define our lives, it is often difficult to hear God's definition. When it is demonstrated how deeply we believe that men should dominate women, it is often difficult to accept God's definition. When we see how much we favor the rich and despise the poor, we cannot fathom God's definition that shows no partiality. When we are told that sexual orientation is not nearly as defining as we think it is, we think that God's definition is too permissive, and we turn out to be grumpy like that elder brother who could not believe that his father was so foolish in throwing a party for his brother who had returned from a far country.

We experience this often at Oakhurst, this sense that the powers of the world tell us who is "in" and who is "out." White folk have long held the idea that we are the inner circle, the modern-day James and John who seek to sit at the right hand of Jesus. Black folk wonder whether white folk are really human beings at all. Nibs had this brought home to him in a conversation with a black seminary student who was doing intern work at Oakhurst. She had a heightened consciousness concerning the need for African Americans to affirm their heritage, and he wondered why she had chosen Oakhurst as her placement rather than a more Afro-centric church. She replied that she wanted to see if white people could really be saved, if there was a shred of humanity left in them that God could redeem. Nibs was grateful for her honesty, and it came home to him in a clear and chilling way that many black folk had the same opinion of white folk that white folk have of black folk—and, that black folk at least have good reason to wonder about the humanity of white folk.

Seeing God as the center of life means that people cannot be reduced to racial classification or gender or bank accounts or sexual orientation or nationality. We cross many boundaries at Oakhurst as our mission statement indicates:

Worldly differences fail to separate our folk. Instead, these differences are the threads that the love of Jesus Christ weaves into the one tapestry—Oakhurst Presbyterian Church. We are young woven with old, black with white, male with female, gay and lesbian with straight. We are employed woven with unemployed, poor with comfortable, strong with broken. We are courageous woven with disheartened, able with sick, hurt with healers. The world uses these categories to separate people from one another and to erect barriers between people. Our life together at Oakhurst Presbyterian

Church, however, is a proclamation that people are more than just race, gender, economic class, and sexual orientation. We all find dignity at Oakhurst no matter the category in which society places us. And we celebrate that each difference finds its beauty and its strength in the Oakhurst tapestry.[7]

We have people with Ph.D. degrees sitting next to people who can barely read. We have people who are affluent sitting next to those who depend on their monthly welfare check. Because of our great variety, there are many occasions when each of us and all of us will encounter how deep the categories of the world are in our hearts. And, because of our great variety, we often encounter someone at Oakhurst who sees us as an opponent at worst and as insensitive at best. Men are seen as insensitive by women; white women are seen as insensitive by black people; black people are seen as insensitive by gay and lesbian people; and the cycle goes on in many different directions. Does all this sound complex? Yes, it is, but we do not throw up our hands in resignation. Rather, we rejoice in the opportunity to be in the fires of life, to be in a community where we do not run in fear of the powers nor seek escape because we are ashamed of the gospel. We affirm the complexity, and we laugh at ourselves a lot. We give thanks for the gift of diversity, which can keep us centered on God.

We recognize the dual nature of this first principle that God is at the center of life. It is a guiding light, a warmth that undergirds and sustains us, but it is also a searing light that exposes those places where the powers still seek to control our lives. We give thanks for the God who loves us and saves us, for the God who calls us as daughters and as sons. We understand the radical equality that stands behind this first principle that God is the center of life, an equality expressed so well by Martin Luther King Jr. in his sermon "The Drum Major Instinct," preached at Ebenezer Baptist Church two months before he was assassinated:

And so Jesus gave us a new norm of greatness. If you want to be important—wonderful. If you want to be recognized—wonderful. If you want to be great—wonderful. But recognize that he who is greatest among you shall be your servant. That's your definition of greatness. And this morning, the thing that I like about it . . . by giving that definition of greatness, it means that everybody can be great. Because everybody can serve. You don't have to have a college degree to serve. You don't have to know about Plato and Aristotle to serve. You don't have to know Einstein's theory of relativity to serve. You don't have to know the second theory of thermodynamics in physics to serve. You only need a heart full of grace. A soul generated by love. And you can be that servant.[8]

We have many differences among ourselves at Oakhurst. We affirm, and we experience, the radical grace of God that acknowledges our diversity and that seeks to unify us in the midst of it. God at the center of our lives is good news for us at Oakhurst. It is a gift that enables us to receive our true humanity as children of God and to see others as children of God, first and foremost. It is a gift that enables us to celebrate our unity as children of God not by obliterating our differences but rather by working with God's Spirit to weave them into the tapestry of life. Diversity becomes a gift, not a problem—a vehicle into the beloved community.

God Likes Diversity

The second guiding principle for our life at Oakhurst is that God likes diversity and offers it to us as a gift, a life-saving and soul-saving gift. When one looks around at the world and its creatures, it ought to be obvious that, if there is a Creator, the Creator likes diversity. The world is a symphony of many sounds, sights, creatures, and cultures, but we often have turned it into a cacophony that produces only alienation and conflict. We have certainly done that in the West in regard to racial categories in which different cultures are seen in hierarchical order rather than in partnership. As we shall see in chapter 3, our emphasis on dividing people into "races" has caused us to see diversity and difference as threatening rather than as cause for celebration. At Oakhurst we seek to affirm the diversity that God has created. We do this not by seeking to wipe out the differences—instead, we celebrate the diversity and seek to make a tapestry out of it.

This second principle affirms that God intends for us to build community on this foundation of diversity. We are afraid of diversity in this country because we have accepted the definitions of the system of racial classification. Because we have so little practice at crossing the boundaries set by race, we are afraid to look for the humanity and the gifts of the "other." What if we saw diversity as a gift rather than a problem? What if we saw it as an opportunity for learning more about God's love and for sharing and receiving the news of God's love? This principle seems obvious and sounds simple, yet it is profound and difficult. In following it, we are not seeking to change the world outside of us but rather to change the world inside of our own selves. We seek to change our ways of perceiving the "other." In this sense, it is both simple and profound. Only our perceptions change—nothing changes, yet everything changes.

We affirm this second principle early in our worship service. We have many different kinds of people who gather together for worship. People from thirteen different countries. People from many racial categories, people of differing educational levels and economic levels, people of different sexual orientations. In other words, we bring many of the categories of the world with us as we come to worship. Soon after our opening hymn, we have a time called the Ritual of Friendship, when people in the congregation greet one another. They not only turn in their pews to shake hands with the person next to them; they get up and really greet one another, moving across the sanctuary to hug and shake hands and acknowledge one another and give thanks for being in one another's presence.

We seek in this time of greeting to create new space for worship in the sanctuary itself and in our hearts. Most of us will greet or touch someone whom we would likely avoid out in the world. Worshipers will touch and be greeted by someone that the world tells them is an enemy. We affirm in this part of worship that God is turning enemies into friends. We affirm in a concrete way the diversity that God has created—we touch the flesh of someone different from us, someone the society has proclaimed to be our enemy. In this way, we proclaim new space in worship—we are asked to leave behind the categories of the world and to experience the new reality that God has created in Jesus Christ. We seek to "embody" in flesh and blood the body of Christ. And, though we know we will continue to carry the categories of the world in our hearts, we seek to help our imaginations experience and consider the new reality.

This greeting time can take several minutes, and it has lengthened our worship service. Initially, it elicited complaints from people who considered it superfluous and even derogatory to worship. On one level, it seemed to break the solemnity and dignity of worship. We agreed that it did break the sense of silent solemnity, but we argued that it actually enhanced the dignity of worship because it was a centering moment that helped us get ready to receive the gifts of God. The complaints have largely faded as the genuine warmth and transforming power of this ritual has been experienced. This affirmation of God's creation of diversity is now an integral part of our worship. We greet one another as the sisters and brothers that God has made us, seeking to be freed from the grip of the powers that tell us that we are enemies rather than neighbors. People who join as members usually cite this ritual as one of the practices that initially attracted them to Oakhurst.

We affirm this second principle not because we want to win points for being inclusive but because, as good Calvinists, we believe that this diversity is a gift to celebrate and is a check and a balance against human arrogance. We believe that one of the reasons that God has given us diversity is to remind us that our particular history is both important and limiting. As children of God, we all should know our own stories—who we are and how we came to be who we are. Without a sense of personal story, we have no roots and can easily be blown about by any prevailing wind or doctrine. One result of holding onto our own stories, however, is that many of us came to believe that our personal story is *the* story. We discount the experience and the stories of others, making their stories threats to us, especially the stories of those who are markedly different from us. One of God's ways of balancing our tendency towards self-centeredness and towards discounting others is the creation of diversity. By emphasizing the gift of diversity, we lift up the truth that our story is only *part* of the story. In order to gain a glimpse of the whole story, we must hear and learn from the stories of others. We must honor our own stories, but we must honor the stories of others. This approach does not lead to relativism, as so many white people seem to believe. Rather, this approach leads to a deep and rich sense of what it means to be human and what it means to be created in the image of God.

In her book, *The Future of Partnership*, Letty Russell describes this phenomenon as "God's arithmetic," a term adopted from Hans-Ruedi Weber.[9] She emphasizes that God's movement in our lives is to help us discover grace in our individual and collective journeys and that God's movement often comes from encounter and even confrontation with the diverse other. In this encounter, we discover both our woeful inadequacies and our great possibilities through God's commitment to us, seen especially in God's use of the other to challenge us, shape us, and love us. When we gain a glimpse of this movement, of God's use of what we had previously feared, it is staggering. We discover how little we know but how much God wants us to know. In John's Gospel, Jesus proclaims it boldly: "I have come that they might have life, life more abundant than they ever dared to imagine." (John 10:10, paraphrase) Russell sums it up well:

> By the gift of God's grace we, who are neither worthy nor able to form mutual relationships with God and one another, discover the power to love and be loved. In this setting love and commitment shared on behalf of others is multiplied so that partnership not only happens as a gift in our lives but also the gifts appear that make growth in unity possible.[10]

We do seek to celebrate difference in our life together at Oakhurst. The positive side of that celebration is the recognition of great gifts that await us in the encounter with the "other," an encounter in which we seek not to absorb or transform the other but to receive and acknowledge the presence of the other. In this encounter, there is the possibility of deepening spiritual awareness—a growing sense of the necessity of community and a sense of the majesty of God in our lives. The other side of that celebration is a growing awareness of how limited we are, of how much our perceptual and conceptual categories have been shaped by our culture and our own history. Such awareness often is received as negative and bad, but as we indicated earlier, it is rather the stuff of our lives, the realities in which we grow and develop. The discovery of such limits is not a revelation of sin but rather a revelation of the structures of our lives. The sinful part comes from our desire to center life in our own story or in our own culture. Life is multifaceted and multicultural, and the only way to come to terms with that reality is to celebrate difference and to look for the gifts that await us in such a celebration.

Perhaps now is a good time to look at our use of the term "multicultural." It is used in a variety of ways. We use it to denote a context where the differences in cultures are respected and celebrated and a context in which a new sense of reality is sought by this encounter of different cultures. Chuck Foster and Ted Brelsford put it well in their summary of the meaning of the term in the research literature:

> This point has been made in a review of the literature on multicultural education by Sleeter and Grant. They describe how educators and researchers use the term *multicultural* to 1) espouse the value of cultural diversity; 2) promote patterns of interaction that respect human rights and cultural diversity among diverse peoples; 3) advocate alternative life choices for people; 4) affirm the necessity of equal opportunity and justice for all peoples; and 5) promote the equitable distribution of power among diverse ethnic/cultural communities as well as create and maintain social, political and economic relationships to enhance all peoples (Sleeter and Grant, 421–44).[11]

In terms of racial diversity, we center on European and African American cultures but also draw from encounters with Hispanic, Asian American, and Native American cultures. In addition, we seek to grow through encounters with gay and lesbian culture, the feminist and womanist traditions, and the movements for justice. All this diversity is also processed with a variety of levels of education and income and subsequent views of the world that develop from those spheres of influence. Thus by "multicultural" we do not mean a context where the dominant culture allows the presence of other cultures while it seeks to assimilate and transform them, proclaiming its views as the only reality. Rather, we mean a context in which different cultures are acknowledged, where dialogue takes place to weave the different cultures into a new reality—a context in which a new people is made from the many, not by assimilation but by cross-fertilization, in which the differences remain but gifts are received by all.

Difficulty in Accepting and Believing Principles 1 and 2

It is, of course, a perilous journey, a journey in which we often fall back into the pattern of assimilation rather than weave a new sense of reality. Recognition of the perils of this journey brings us to our third guiding principle: we continue to disbelieve the first two principles. In that sense, we seek continually to acknowledge the struggles in our individual and our collective hearts over acceptance that God is the center of life and that God likes diversity. In many ways, we find ourselves in the same position as ancient Israel. We want to worship God, but we also want to worship other gods. Rather than being circles with God at the center, our hearts are more often like ellipses with two centers, and much of the journey of our lives is an attempt to balance these two centers: the voice of God and the voices of the powers.

By "powers" we are referring to the spiritual reality captured in the biblical language concerning "the principalities and the powers." No one expressed the depth of the struggle in our hearts over the powers better than Paul in Eph. 6:10–20, which includes these words:

> Finally, be strong in the Lord and in the strength of his power. Put on the whole armor of God, so that you may be able to stand against the wiles of the devil. For our struggle is not against enemies of blood and flesh, but against the rulers, against the authorities, against the cosmic powers of this present darkness, against the spiritual forces of evil in the heavenly places. Therefore take up the whole armor of God, so that you may be able to withstand on that evil day, and having done everything, to stand firm."[12]

Though we cringe at the "warrior" nature of Paul's metaphors in this text, we affirm strongly the depth of the struggle that Paul depicts here. The definitions of the powers have become intertwined with our own self-definitions, and it is exceedingly difficult to unravel those definitions to allow God's definitions to prevail in our hearts. Like many others, we have benefited greatly from Walter Wink's foundational work that helps us regain the meaning of the biblical language concerning the powers.[13] One of our foundational experiences at Oakhurst is the continuing power of racism in our individual and communal lives. Many of us seek to reject its claim over us and in us, yet it continues to manifest itself in our lives. In this situation, we are encountering the spiritual depths of the powers that Paul describes in Ephesians 6. Wink's discussion of this spiritual reality is helpful:

> What I propose is viewing the spiritual Powers not as separate heavenly or ethereal entities but as *the inner aspect of material or tangible manifestations*

of power. I suggest that the "angels of nature" are the patterning of physical things—rocks, trees, plants, the whole God-glorifying, dancing, visible universe; that the "principalities and powers" are the inner or spiritual essence, or gestalt, of an institution or state or system; that the "demons" are the psychic or spiritual power emanated by organizations or individuals or subaspects of individuals whose energies are bent on overpowering others; that "gods" are the very real archetypal or ideological structures that determine or govern reality and its mirror, the human brain; that the mysterious "elements of the universe" (*stoicheia tou kosmou*) are the invariances (formerly called "laws") which, though often idolized by humans, conserve the self-consistency of each level of reality in its harmonious interrelationship with every other level and the Whole; and that "Satan" is the actual power that congeals around collective idolatry, injustice, or inhumanity, a power that increases or decreases according to the degree of collective refusal to choose higher values.[14]

Wink's interpretation is helpful as we consider our third guiding principle: that acceptance of the first two principles is difficult for us. Who would not accept the great news that God is at the center of our lives? And, why would anyone resist the obvious proclamation that God likes diversity? The biblical language concerning the powers provides insight into these questions. The acceptance of the first two guiding principles is not just a matter of our conscious will. Though it is an important agency in this process, the human will is bound by the imagination. The truth is that the fallen powers of the world have captured our hearts and our imaginations, and until our imaginations are stimulated and expanded, the will is of limited use. When Mark's Gospel tells us that Jesus proclaims that the reign of God is at hand, it is a call to expand our imaginations, to allow ourselves to consider a whole new world, a whole new view of reality that the powers have previously convinced us is unrealistic and naïve.

When Jesus calls on us to "repent" in Mark 1:15, he is not only asking us to change our behavior. He is challenging us to "turn around" and see a new reality, to receive a new vision of who we are and who God is and who the world is. In this sense, the proclamation of a new reality makes it possible for our will even to contemplate a change. When Jesus announces that the God movement is here and now, is available to us now, he is bringing us the possibility of affirming that God is the center of life and of our lives. He is telling us not only that we "ought" to change our lives but that experiencing this new reality will make us want to change our lives. Our shift from being captured by the powers to being followers of Jesus will therefore not be a journey filled with grumpiness, signaling a change made only to avoid eternal punishment, but rather a journey characterized by joy and desire, like that of the Samaritan woman who encounters Jesus at the well in John 4 and who tells him to give her some of that living water. She *wants* that living water. She is empowered by her first taste.

The struggle in our hearts over this third principle means that while we are thirsty for that living water, we often drink junk water to try to quench that thirst. In so doing, we block our own ability to receive or even want the living water that God is offering us in Jesus Christ. Lest this seem hopelessly theoretical and ethereal, we want to offer a concrete example that we will explore more deeply in the next chapter. That example is the power of racism in our lives. Those of us who are white Southerners know its power. We learned racism long before we knew we were learning it. It captured our imaginations long before we had any idea that it was doing so. We were nurtured on the white, Southern view that those classified as "white" were superior to all other racial classifications. It was and continues to be a power in our lives, though it is diminished. We learned it not only from people who seemed mean and cruel but from people who loved us and nurtured us—our families, our churches, our teachers. It captured our imaginations so much that it came as a shock to us when the new vision broke into our consciousness: White people are not superior, and life is not meant to be a hierarchy of domination.

In considering this new reality, many felt disloyal to their families and nurturing communities and to their own identities formed by these communities. Yet many white people began to want this new calling; we began to consider a new identity that disowned racism; we went into conflict with the very ones who had loved us and had given us life. We knew personally the sting of Jesus' words in Luke 12:51: "Do you think I have come to bring peace on earth? No, I tell you, but rather division!" He goes on to talk about dividing family members against one another, and we know that journey well in regard to race. Not only are family members divided, but division also exists in our own inner view of ourselves. We have been willing to tolerate the ambiguity of this journey on race because we have been given a view of that new world, and we have come to desire it.

It is that desire that makes us able to tolerate the conflict within ourselves and with others. It is that longing that causes us to listen and receive the gifts that are offered when others expose the continuing power of racism in our lives. In this sense, the vision of the new reality of the God movement is ever before us, calling us into new life. This vision is always in tension with the knowledge of how much we will continue to resist the new life because our hearts and our imaginations have been captured by the powers of the world. In order to grow into the new life, we must acknowledge how much we resist that growth, how much we need God's continuing commitment to us in order to grow, and how much we need the diverse community to teach us and discipline us. In our life together at Oakhurst, we must keep before us at all times the vision of the new life and the continuing power of the categories of the world.

An important decision early in our tenure as pastors demonstrated this tension. When we came to Oakhurst, our choir director was a white seminary student from Candler School of Theology at Emory University. He was an excellent choir director for us—he began to broaden our base of music, adding to our repertoire *Songs of Zion*, an African American songbook from the United Methodist Church. His time as a student came to an end, however, and he accepted a call as pastor of another church. We began to search for a new choir director, and we developed a diverse search committee, chaired by a white woman who is a skilled musician.

We interviewed several candidates, and the clear choice was a black man who had great skills and impeccable credentials. Rather than feeling elated at the possibility, I felt anxiety, as we prepared to take this recommendation to the session, our local church's governing body. The source of my anxiety was not whether we could afford him but whether his race would matter—Oakhurst had never had a black choir director.

The session meeting demonstrated that my anxiety was not fantasy. Ten of our twelve elders attended, six white and four black. The white woman who had chaired the search committee brought the report and indicated that the recommendation was that we hire our first African American choir director. Many questions were asked about his qualifications, his salary, and the type of music he would be playing. We never got a direct comment about his racial classification, but when the vote was taken, the intentions became clear. The first vote ended in a five-to-five tie, without a vote from Nibs, who was moderating the meeting. The five voting against the recommendation were all white. The five voting for it were the four black elders and the white chair of the search committee.

We voted a second time, with the same results, except that this time Nibs voted for the recommendation. The motion passed six to five, and by the narrowest of margins we had hired one of the best organists and choir directors in the Atlanta area. It was a lesson about the tensions inherent in seeking to live the new life while still holding on to the old definitions. Moreover, God laughed at us, for none of us got exactly what we had voted for. Our first African American choir director did not like gospel music, and his taste in music was actually much closer to the white people who voted against him than to the black people who voted for him. It was as if God was mocking us as we tentatively and gingerly tried to step into the new life, all the while clinging to the old.

Three biblical passages serve as guides for us as we seek both to acknowledge our continuing resistance to God's movement in our lives and to delight and grow into that movement. In Exod. 20:2–3, at the beginning of the Ten Commandments, God speaks these words: "I am the LORD your God, who brought you out of the land of Egypt, out of the house of slavery; you shall have no other gods before me." The commandments begin in a great gift: freedom from slavery, and in them God gives guidance to the Israelites concerning the way to keep their newly given freedom. It is not unwarranted guidance, for the Israelites have already longed to return to the security and the slavery of Egypt: "If only we had died by the hand of the LORD in the land of Egypt, when we sat by the fleshpots and ate our fill of bread. . . ." (Exod. 16:3).

God knows our hearts, so God offers guidance when we are tempted to slip back into slavery. The first guiding rule is central: "You shall have no other gods before me." This commandment not only refers to the wooden or clay figures fashioned into gods—it also refers to the powers that shape us and that we shape into idols and allow to rule our lives and to capture our imaginations. We come to believe that materialism is at the heart of life, that economic forces are ultimate, that money can save us. So we spend most of our energy trying to balance the God we know in Jesus with the god we know in materialism. We are taught that race is central and that white people are superior, and we cannot imagine a world in which equality is affirmed and power is shared. We have learned that men are superior and should dominate women, and we are shocked to hear women talk of their own experience that doesn't need to be validated by men. We call it blasphemy when women seek images of God from their own experience. There are many other examples of this process, but these should give a view of our orientation to the First Commandment—it reminds us that when we allow the powers of the world to define us and to become idols, we risk returning to slavery and enslaving others. God wants us to celebrate our freedom rather than return to the slavery of Egypt. Paul understands this in his words to the Galatians (5:1): "Freedom is what we have. Christ has set us free. Stand, then, as free people, and do not allow yourselves to become slaves again." (TEV) We often use this as a benediction in worship.

Paul's words in Romans serve as the second biblical passage that helps us as we seek to find our way through these three guiding principles. As we indicated earlier, our life in multicultural ministry has given us a much better appreciation of Paul's context and struggles as he seeks to be a witness for the emerging church in a new world. We use the words of his writings often in this book, and we find his struggles enlightening as we remember that he, too, was being dragged across cultural boundaries by the power of the Spirit as the circle of faith was widened to include the Gentiles. In relation to the struggle to live in the new vision while remaining in the grip of the old life, his words in Rom. 7:15 are startling: "I do not understand my own actions. For I do not do what I want, but I do the very thing I hate."

This struggle is reflected in our third guiding principle at Oakhurst: we want very much to live in the new vision, but we often find ourselves opting for the old life, having learned and accepted the definitions of the world about race, gender, money, and many other categories. Paul emphasizes in Rom. 7:20 that the principalities and powers are so deeply interwoven with the fabric of our lives and with our institutions that he calls this force the "sin that dwells with me." Paul has a profound recognition that following Jesus is not just about ourselves—it is about how we see others and see ourselves. The sin that dwells within us is not some alien being—it is the very fallen order of the powers that shaped our understanding of ourselves from our very beginning, long before we had any idea that we were receiving it. Indeed, it is what Paul means by "flesh." Not our bodies, not our sexuality, not our historicity, but rather our very perceptual apparatus, learned from family and friends—this is "flesh."

Lest we sink in despair because we seem so mired in the "flesh," so inextricably bound up with the powers that we cannot find life, Jesus bursts upon the scene to proclaim a whole new reality, a whole new way of seeing ourselves and the world. It is the movement of God into our lives, the movement that enables us to have hope where despair seems only logical, that calls us to leap for joy rather than lament in the dirge of death. Jesus shared and lived this message with the women and men who followed him. In the twelfth chapter of Luke, he affirms a life-giving message to his followers: "Don't be afraid, little flock—it is God's good pleasure to move into your lives." God takes pleasure in bringing us life—astonishingly good news! Prior to this, Jesus has shared the famous words about not being anxious, for God can be trusted. In Matthew's version in 6:24, Jesus adds, "No one can serve two masters; for a slave will either hate the one and love the other or be devoted to the one and despise the other. You cannot serve God and wealth."

In these verses, Jesus offers us both analysis and hope. We often try to balance the gods in our lives. We do try to serve two masters, and in our balancing act, we end up dominated by fear and anxiety, fearful that God will crush us for being unfaithful, and anxious because the other gods promise life but deliver death. Into this journey comes the power and promise of "God with us." Even as we have trouble believing that God is at the center, even as we dismiss the diversity that God has created, God continues to move into our lives and call us out of death into life.

It is the call of this God movement that is the center of our lives together at Oakhurst. As we have made clear already, we often wander from our center at Oakhurst, but we are always being called back to the One who is our east and our west, our north and our south. The great good news of life at Oakhurst is that it is our very diversity—a diversity that seems so troubling and unsettling at times—that keeps us open to being disciplined and called back to the center. This diversity and our seeking to value it in our structures is at the heart of Oakhurst's being a remarkable place. We have been truly blessed by what we feared and what we continue, at times, to fear. In the midst of our fears, God has blessed us.

Chapter Three

A Primer on Race

*I*f diversity is such a gift and such a powerful vehicle of grace, why are we so afraid of it? Why do neighborhoods change because of it? Why do we see it as such an enemy? The answer for the American context is, in a word, race. We spend considerable time in this chapter on race so that we can better understand why multicultural ministry is so rare and so difficult. But we will also come to see the many gifts that await us in multicultural ministry. Race has been at the heart of our national life since the Europeans came here, taking the land from the natives and bringing Africans and Asians in to work the land. Race remains at the center of our national life—it is one of the central American themes. All communities of faith must come to terms with the system of race and the racism that is part of that system, especially those communities that are multicultural or that seek to be multicultural. Unless we travel through the land of race, our efforts will be little more than the dominant culture's seeking blessing by adding other ethnic groups without having to seek partnership with those groups.

Race is the lens through which we embrace American life. From the European beginnings of this nation, race has defined us, directed us, and separated us. It has always been the great divide. It has separated us from ourselves and from one another. It has left all of us feeling homeless, lost and drifting without a safe harbor to call home. Although those classified as "nonwhite" by the system of race have suffered much more deeply than those classified as "white," all of us have scars and are in danger of losing our humanity because of the power of race. To one degree or another we are all lost and do not know how to find our way home. This chapter is about finding our way home, and it describes a journey that can be both profound and painful.

The journey of Jacob seeking to go home can be instructive as we consider our own stories and journeys. This part of Jacob's journey can be found in

Gen. 25–33. Jacob has a twin brother named Esau. Esau was the first-born son, a position of honor, but he was born with his brother Jacob grabbing at his heel. Esau became a hunter who was favored by his father Isaac. Jacob, the younger son, was favored by his mother Rebekah.

In Gen. 27, we read that Isaac, who was now blind, called Esau in to ask him to prepare a favorite meal so that Isaac could give him his blessing as the elder son. Esau went out to hunt game for the meal. Rebekah had overheard the conversation, and while Esau was out hunting, she helped Jacob prepare a meal and take it in to her husband, Isaac. Jacob, disguised as Esau, went in to his father. Isaac, unable to see, told his visitor that he smelled like Esau but sounded like Jacob. "Who are you, my son?" he asked. Jacob lied and said, "I am Esau." By this deceit, Jacob received the blessing intended for Esau. Esau soon returned and brought the meal to his father, at which time he heard the terrible news that Jacob had stolen his blessing. Isaac and Esau lamented the loss, and Esau resolved to kill his brother after the death of his father. Jacob learned of Esau's anger and fled in terror. He went to live with his mother's brother Laban. He sojourned for many years and learned the ways of the world from his cunning uncle.

In Gen. 31 and 32, we find Jacob as a grown, mature man. Later on, he would come to be the father of the Twelve Tribes of Israel, but to do this, he first had to return home. He had been in flight for many years, and he was tired of wrestling with Laban. Moreover, he had had a dream in which God told him to go home. God told Jacob that God would make a great nation from Jacob's children. Jacob longed to go home, to find peace, to come to terms with his past and put an end to his flight. He had lied to his father—he had stolen from his brother. His past was weighing heavily on him, and he wanted to go home. But, before he could go home to his father's land, he first had to pass through the land of his brother Esau, the brother whom he had cheated.

Jacob hoped for the best. Genesis tells us that Jacob sent messengers ahead to his brother Esau, telling Esau that he was coming home and that he must pass through Esau's land. He also let Esau know how rich he had become. He even listed his assets—all the goats, rams, bulls, and cows. His messengers returned to Jacob with terrible news: Esau was coming to meet Jacob and was bringing four hundred men with him. Jacob was scared to death. It was payback time.

If you know the story of Jacob, you know that he was cunning. He devised a couple of plans to try to mitigate Esau's anger and destructive power. First, he would try to overwhelm Esau with gifts. Thus, he sent wave after wave after wave of people with presents for Esau, telling Esau that Jacob was close behind. This is the way that wealthy people and societies often try to end their problems and crises. If we just throw enough money at the problem, it will be solved.

Jacob prayed for deliverance, but his prayer was a flight from, rather than a recognition of, responsibility. Jacob's prayer in Gen. 32 emphasizes God's responsibility for Jacob's predicament. Jacob muttered a few words about his unworthiness, but the tone of his prayer was intended to remind God that all of this was God's responsibility. This was God's doing, the prayer insists; God must provide deliverance from Esau's power.

Nowhere in his prayer did Jacob say the truth—that he had sinned against his family. He had lied to his father and cheated his brother. He had brought destruction and disaster upon himself. He did not say, "God, I've made a terrible mess—please save me!" Instead, he blamed God for the problem and asked God to get him out of it. Jacob believed that his brother Esau was his biggest problem. If he could just find a way to get around Esau—maybe bribe him with all these presents, maybe have a great escape by splitting up his company, maybe ask God to deliver him. If he could just get around Esau, his problem would be solved.

Jacob's problem was not Esau, however. His biggest problem was himself. Jacob was unwilling to face his own brokenness and destructiveness. In all of his scheming and praying, Jacob was unable to discern the truth. He was unable to see that what prevented him from going home was not Esau but rather his own refusal to accept responsibility for his predicament. After all, it might have been his mother Rebekah's fault. Remember, she had helped him in the deception. She told him what to do, to put on Esau's "manly" clothing of the hunter. So, it was really his mother's fault. If she hadn't asked him to do it, he wouldn't have done it. Or, maybe it was Esau's fault. Esau had sold his birthright to Jacob—sold it cheaply, too, for a bowl of soup. Didn't that show how lightly Esau regarded everything? So Esau planted this deception in Jacob's heart. If Esau had said, "No" to the deal, Jacob surely would have stopped. Or, maybe it was God's fault. If God hadn't asked Jacob to go home in that dream, Jacob would have remained in comfort, near Laban. As his prayer indicates, Jacob was still in flight. Even though he was headed home, he was still running away.

Yet God was gracious to Jacob, just as God often is to us when we are broken and fleeing in anxiety and blaming God for our problem. Jacob found his answer not in being delivered from facing Esau but in being forced to face himself. Jacob settled down for the night. He sent everybody away from him. He needed to think about all of this—to wrestle with it. The scriptural story in Genesis tells us that Jacob was left alone and someone came to wrestle with him in the middle of the night. It is in the nighttime that we often wrestle with our problems and with who we are. Nighttime wrestling comes when we seek sleep; nighttime wrestling comes just when we seek to find home.

So it was with Jacob. Alone and frightened, he wrestled in the middle of the night about his identity. It is not clear who came to wrestle him. It is not clear whether it was a dream or whether it actually happened outside Jacob's own psyche, but in this wrestling Jacob found an authentic answer to his problem. The wrestling was fierce and painful. It lasted until the break of day. The easy and quick healing for which Jacob had hoped was not a possibility.

During the struggle, Jacob cried out to be blessed, "I will not let you go until you bless me." It was a calling back to the very lie itself, to the first time he had come to his blind father to receive the blessing of his elder brother—by theft. Now, for a second time Jacob was asking for a blessing: "Give me a blessing, or I will not let you go!" Once again, he heard the same question: "Who are you? Give me your name." This time Jacob did not say Esau, as he had said the first time. This time he gave his true name: "My name is Jacob." To give his name was to speak of his past and of his deception. He received a blessing this time by being himself, by claiming his past and by claiming responsibility. To be blessed, to return home, Jacob had to give his name. He had to accept responsibility for who he was and what he had done. . . . And, for this he was wounded forever.

Yet giving his real name did not lead to death as he had thought it would. He was not destroyed; he was wounded. As a matter of fact, he was changed. Because he had given his name and acknowledged his brokenness, Jacob was able to find his way home—not as an innocent person, not as a good person, but as one who had seen God face-to-face, had seen himself face-to-face . . . and had been spared. Jacob had wrestled with his sinfulness, his brokenness, and his lostness. In claiming his own self and responsibility for himself, he did not find obliteration as he had thought he would. Instead he found the way home. He found mercy and forgiveness.[1]

The journey through the land of race will be such a journey for many, especially those who have been claimed by the name "white" and who have claimed the name "white." To encounter the power of the system of race in our lives and our participation in it is painful, but it is the only way home. We use the term "the system of race" for this central and defining theme because our working premise is that the purpose of racial classification has never been to divide the human family into different branches, much as one analyzes butterflies or roses. Rather, the purpose of racial classification is to determine who has access to power and who does not. Using racial classification is not intended to divide the human family into different ethnic groups but rather to say that there are only two groups that matter: those classified as "white" and those classified as "nonwhite." Thus those classified as "nonwhite' are often called "racial/ethnic" groups, as if to say that those classified as white are not "racial/ethnic," thus insuring a fundamental and qualitative difference between "white' and "nonwhite." As we shall see in this chapter, those two groups are not nearly as fixed as it might appear. They are indeed fluid, changing, amorphous groups, but they are useful as analytical tools, and they have been powerful categories in American history.

Our working definition of "race" is as follows:

> RACE—A political concept often alleged to be scientific. Its purpose is to divide the family of humanity into two categories: "white" and "nonwhite." The purpose of the division is to determine who will have access to power and who will not. The modern concept of race was born in the European desire to control people in other countries and their assets. It is an arbitrary and political concept, like Democrat and Republican.[2]

This working definition does not seek to melt away cultural or ethnic differences in order to make everybody the same. Rather, it seeks to overcome the system of race by affirming that there is a common humanity that undergirds and connects us all. This definition seeks to acknowledge the fundamental inequity that underlies modern racial classification and asks us to reconsider both the modern racial classification system and the resulting categories of "race." We are asked to do this revisioning so that we can affirm our common humanity rather than support the hierarchy of race, which posits that white folks are normal and should be on top while the "racial/ethnics" are mutations and should be under white control.

When we use this approach with various groups in workshops on racism, some strongly react and argue that the system of race is objective and that the scientists who originally envisioned it were interested in analytical knowledge rather than domination. Here is not the place to discuss this debate of metascience, but we usually emphasize that whatever one decides about the origin of racial classification, one must agree that it has evolved into a system whose goal and purpose is domination. We do not seek to besmirch the good name of science but rather to encourage understanding concerning how the system has been and continues to be used. We must note, however, that even the early "scientific" descriptions of the racial categories contain some interesting language for a discipline that seeks to be rational and objective. One of the first systems of racial classification came in 1738 from a giant in the classification of plants and animals, the Swedish scientist Carolus Linnaeus:

Homo Americanus—Tenacious, contented, free; ruled by custom.
Homo Eurpoaeus—Light, lively, inventive; ruled by rites.
Homo Asiaticus—Stern, haughty, stingy; ruled by opinion.
Homo After—Cunning, slow, negligent; ruled by caprice.[3]

Fifty years later in 1785, in *Notes on Virginia*, the great American egalitarian Thomas Jefferson writes on the different races. Jefferson's powerful prose has helped to define the American identity: "We hold these truths to be self-evident, that all men are created equal." This radical idea of equality has been the driving force behind many of the justice movements in our nation's history, including those that have insisted that women are included in this idea of equality. Thomas Jefferson definitely caught the American pulse and impulse in the Declaration of Independence. Writing in 1785, however, he doesn't express the certainty of equality that fired the vision of the Declaration. In his *Notes on Virginia* he begins to see a hierarchy in this circle of equality, predating George Orwell's concept that while all humans are created equal, some humans are more equal than others.[4] In his scientific analysis, Jefferson puts the "Homo sapiens Europaeus" on top of the racial ladder, with the "Indian" next and "blacks" on the bottom. While hoping to be objective and scientific, Jefferson admits that much more study is needed, yet he must add this conclusion:

I advance it, therefore, as a suspicion only, that the blacks, whether originally a distinct race, or made distinct by time and circumstances, are inferior to the whites in the endowments both of body and mind.[5]

Although Jefferson later expresses misgivings about his dismissal of the equality of black people, his ruminations reflect the difficulty of all those who are classified "white" in our society; we may want to be committed to the idea of equality, but we also prefer the economic privileges of the inequality of race.[6] For instance, Jefferson's highlighting of the potential equality of "Indian" did not prevent one of his successors as president, Andrew Jackson, from forcibly removing the Cherokees from north Georgia after gold was discovered there. Moreover, Jackson removed them in defiance of a Supreme Court order forbidding their removal, in a campaign that came to be known as the "Trail of Tears."[7] For all of his misgivings about slavery, Thomas Jefferson yet benefited immensely from it. At his death, his will freed only five of his slaves, all from the Hemmings family.[8]

We are not trying to attack Thomas Jefferson in these brief comments about his struggle as a prime example of the continuing American dilemma over race. While many of us who are classified as "white" would like to disavow race and racism, we still benefit immensely from it. Jefferson was in the middle of this same struggle, even as he quoted "scientific" evidence that seemed to verify that Africans were inferior to Europeans. And, if Africans were less equal than Europeans, then the "self-evident" clause of the Declaration of Independence doesn't apply to them and maybe, just maybe, holding them in bondage might be justified. In one form or another, "white" folk have gone through the same process as Jefferson did in order to justify the many privileges that come to us because we are classified as "white" under the system of race.

When we do workshops on racism, we often begin by asking people to call out the names of the racial classifications. The answers are always varied and intriguing. Usually we get categories like these: white, black, African American, European, Caucasian, Hispanic, Latino, Native American, Asian, Pacific Islander, African, Mongoloid, Negroid, Oriental, Mid-Eastern, Eskimo, Arabic, Indian. The list is virtually endless, but then we begin to discuss the list and the origins of the various categories. Several things are noted—the names are usually based in colors and geography and culture. The categories are fluid and evoking, and often seem arbitrary. In terms of colors, the use of "white" and "black" is illuminating. We note that those designated as "white" are actually not white at all—they are rather various shades of pink and peach and rust. Those designated as "black" are actually not black at all—they are usually various shades of brown and tan. Why use "white" and "black" then? Because of their use in the English language— "white" usually means "pure," "good," and "holy" while "black" usually means "bad," "evil," and "dangerous." White is the color worn by brides at weddings to denote purity while black is the color often worn at funerals to denote mourning and death.

By this time in the workshops, there is usually some squirming by "white" folks and growing attention by "nonwhite" folks. We note how fluid the categories are. When we were growing up, there were only three racial groups noted—Caucasoid, Mongoloid, and Negroid. In the 2000 census, however, there were over seventeen! We also note the arbitrary nature of the terms. "Caucasian" usually means people of European descent, but not all Europeans have always been included in this category. Indeed, people of Irish descent were legally defined as "non-white" in the early history of Virginia.[9] We also note that the term "Asian" is geographical but that usually only people from far-east Asia (Japan, China, Vietnam, Korea, etc.) are classified as "Asian." Darker people from other parts of Asia, such as Pakistan, Sri Lanka, and India are often not visualized as "Asian." We note also that people classified as "Hispanic" are not from Spain but are from Central and South America. "Hispanic" comes from "Hispanola," the Latin term from the Iberian Peninsula of Spain and Portugal, but it does not describe folk who live there.

It soon becomes apparent that the system of racial classification is fluid, arbitrary, and not scientific. Why, then, do we use it? Why have we used it for over three hundred years in America, even though it is always changing? The system of racial classification, for all its fluidity and arbitrary nature, stays in place because its purpose is not to classify the different branches of the human family but to act as a gatekeeper, as a dividing line between those who have access to power and privilege and those who do not. In this sense, at the heart of racial classification only two categories are important, no matter how many permutations there are in any given era: "white" and "nonwhite." Those classified as "white" have access to power and privilege. Those classified as "nonwhite" have little access to power and privilege, and any access that is gained comes at a great cost.

The purpose of the system of race that has developed in the West is to segregate "white" people from the rest of humanity, separating them out as special, as more intelligent, as more capable of being in charge. Whether or not this intent was there from the beginning of racial classification in the West is not as important as agreement that the system has come to be used in that way.[10] "White" has come to be seen as normal and normative, and all other "races" must spend their time and energy seeking to act like white people if they want access to power and privilege. The categories of racial classification, then, turn out not to be biological or genetic at all. They turn out to be social constructs, political categories that indicate distribution of power. Few scientists today consider these categories biologically scientific—the science community has left "race" behind as a meaningful biological concept. There may be a need to describe the various ethnicities of the human family, but biological "race" is not it. And, given the history of the use of "race," in which a hierarchy of humanity has developed rather than a circle of cultures, it may be well to leave off any such classifications for a long time.

Because of the system of race and its segregation of "white" people from all other humans, those classified as "white" have a difficult time receiving diversity as a gift. White people see other cultures as a severe threat to their way of life. White people have been taught and have accepted the idea that they are superior to all others, that other "races" are not like them, that other "races" will dilute them and weaken them and bring them harm. For this reason, public school integration has by and large been a failure. White people simply do not believe and seem not to want to believe that their children will get a good education if there are many black children in the class. For this reason, neighborhoods seem to change overnight after a few black or Hispanic families move in. They change not because blacks and Hispanic people move in but because white folk flee from the presence of those that the system of race has taught them are inferior and dangerous.

If we are to develop multicultural communities and places of worship, this fear and aversion must be put on the table and acknowledged, or we will never make progress. It is essential to acknowledge how deeply imbedded in white consciousness is the fear of "people of color." Thomas Edsall cites one clear example of the depth of this belief with a report seeking to explain why Democratic voters near Detroit had made a dramatic shift in voting patterns for president. In 1960, the district went 63 percent to 37 percent for Democrat John Kennedy over Republican Richard Nixon. In 1984, there was almost a complete reversal, with 63 percent going to Republican Ronald Reagan and 33 percent for Democrat Walter Mondale. The study explained the shift in blunt terms:

> These white Democratic defectors express a profound distaste for blacks, a sentiment that pervades almost everything they think about government and politics. . . . Blacks constitute the explanation for their [white defectors'] vulnerability and for almost everything that has gone wrong in their lives; not being black is what constitutes being middle class; not living with blacks is what makes a neighborhood a decent place to live. These sentiments have important implications for Democrats, as virtually all progressive symbols and theses have been redefined in racial and pejorative terms. . . . The special status of blacks is perceived by almost all of these individuals as a serious obstacle to their personal advancement. Indeed, discrimination against whites has become a well-assimilated and ready explanation for their status, vulnerability and failures. . . . Ronald Reagan's image [was] formed against this [Democratic] backdrop—disorder and weakness, passivity, and humiliation and a party that failed to speak for the average person. By contrast, Reagan represented a determined consistency and an aspiration to unity and pride.[11]

This report accentuates why white folk have such a difficult time receiving diversity as a gift. From the "white" point of view, diversity is a powerful and painful threat, not a gift that enhances life.

This fear of diversity is not confined to white people, however. It also lives in the hearts of those considered nonwhite, though not nearly as deeply as in the hearts of white people. As white people, we are on dangerous ground here as we seek to describe some of the nonwhite experience. One of the arrogant fallacies of the system of race is that those classified as white believe that we are the center of life and that we know the humanity of others whom we have classified as less human than we are. The stunning truth for whites is that we know very little of the humanity of those "others" partly because those classified as nonwhite choose not to reveal their humanity to those classified as white. This decision is made out of the desire to survive in a hostile landscape.

Although black people and others classified as nonwhite in this society are human beings, they are told that they are not human in the same way that white people are human—that they are part of the lesser order. They are told that there is something wrong with them and their cultures. This dissonance produces great tension in those classified as nonwhite. They learn that white people cannot be trusted and that their lives and their humanity are at risk if they let white people into their space. This dissonance makes people classified as nonwhite want to hide themselves from white people, to disengage from white people. It produces great anger and frustration and a dualism born of the need to live as a human being in a society that tells them that they are not human beings. Although they must be in the midst of white people in this society, they are wary of letting white people into their lives. This dualism is nothing new for people classified as nonwhite. W. E. B. DuBois lifted it up as well as anyone:

> One feels his two-ness—an American, a Negro, two souls, two thoughts, two unreconciled strivings, two warring ideals in one dark body. . . .
>   The history of the American Negro is the history of this strife—this longing to attain self-conscious manhood, to merge his double self into a better and truer self. . . . He would not Africanize America for America has too much to teach the world and Africa. He would not bleach the Negro soul in a flood of white Americanism, for he knows that Negro blood has a message for the world. He simply wishes to make it possible for a man to be both a Negro and an American, without being cursed and spit upon.[12]

This dualism is at the heart of the system of race. People classified as nonwhite feel and act like human beings, but they are told by society that they are not. The institutions of white society reflect it; those classified as nonwhite who act like human beings are criticized, ostracized, ridiculed, persecuted, and executed. Throughout our nation's history, most white people have been unwilling and at times unable to tolerate nonwhite people acting like real people in their presence. Because of this situation, people classified as nonwhite have been forced to decide on how to survive in a hostile environment. Many have chosen the dualism described by DuBois, surviving by keeping a huge gap between themselves and white folks.

Some have survived at an even greater price; they have internalized the oppression. They have come to believe the white view of their lack of humanity in order to survive in a white world. In every age, nonwhite people have sought to affirm their humanity again and again, but the power of the system and the need to survive have caused some to believe the lies of the system of race. No one said it more clearly than did Malcolm X:

> We hated our heads, we hated the shape of our nose, we wanted one of those dog-like noses, you know; we hated the color of our skin, hated the blood of Africa that was in our veins. And in hating our features and our skin and our blood, why we had to end up hating ourselves. Our color became to us a chain—we felt it was holding us back; our color became to us like a prison which we felt was keeping us confined, not letting us go this way or that way. We felt that all of these restrictions were based solely upon our color, and the psychological reaction to that would have to be that as long as we felt imprisoned or chained or trapped by black skin, black features, and black blood, that skin and those features and that blood holding us back automatically had to become hateful to us. It made us feel inferior; it made us feel inadequate; made us feel helpless.[13]

It would be wonderful if this process were ancient history, purged and eradicated with the civil rights movement. Yet it is still with us, as these words from a "conservative" black author testified:

> Even to this day I have a tiny fear that one day I will open a newspaper and find, printed for all the world to see, the story of some nerdy scientist who has uncovered undeniable proof that black people are innately inferior to every other race. I can see the headlines now: "German Scientist Wins Nobel Prize for Genetic Discoveries Proving the Inferior Status of the Black Race." And the lead paragraph will explain that his findings have been confirmed by a team of scientists hand-picked by the NAACP.[14]

In this storm, nonwhite people often choose from several options for survival, often balancing the options in their own individual and collective spirits. One option is the internalized oppression described so well by Malcolm X. It exists as many forms in which the white model of life is accepted as the norm, and all others are seen as a diminished version. The idea that the problems of nonwhite peoples come not from injustice but from their own deficiencies is one form of this internalized oppression.

A poignant moment in this regard came a couple of years ago when one of our African American members came to see us. We consider ourselves privileged that African Americans will allow us to be their pastors and thus make themselves vulnerable to white people, taking a leap of faith over the great divide of race. This particular member was hurt and angry because he had discovered that hard work and a middle-class lifestyle would not make him acceptable to white people. He had thought that if he succeeded in the white world, then the power of racial classification would disappear, but it had recently been made clear to him that race would always matter in a white-dominated society—no matter how successful he was.

This most dangerous deception of the system of race—that those called nonwhite can gain some measure of humanity by working hard and succeeding—seeks to shift responsibility for the system's injustice from the white people who created it to the nonwhite people who were declared inferior by it. The system of race thus posits that what seems to be racism is really not that at all but rather the natural and correct reaction to the fact that nonwhite people are inferior and less worthy. Those nonwhite people who accept this view—and many more accept it than we want to admit—suffer from internalized oppression. They have come to believe that lies told by racism are true.

Another alternative for survival is separatism, in which nonwhite people seek to protect themselves and their identities by having as little engagement with white people as possible. They choose separatism not because their psyches are fragile but because white people seem so incorrigible, so unable even to consider the humanity of others. This perception is one of the reasons that the worship hour tends to remain segregated. Nonwhite folks do not want to mess with white folks, do not want to have to justify their worship style and do not want to have to accept the white idea of reality. From Henry McNeal Turner to Marcus Garvey to the Nation of Islam, this alternative has been especially part of the dialogue in the black community. It is born out of a desire to affirm the humanity of black people and out of a decision, based on centuries of struggle with white structures, that white people will not give up their racism. This pessimism is reflected by Derrick Bell:

> Consider: In this last decade of the twentieth century, color determines the social and economic status of all African Americans, both those who have been highly successful and their poverty-bound brethren whose lives are grounded in misery and despair. We rise and fall less as a result of our efforts than in response to the needs of a white society that condemns all blacks to quasi citizenship as surely as it segregated our parents and enslaved their forebears. The fact is that, despite what we designate as progress wrought through struggle over many generations, we remain what we were in the beginning: a dark and foreign presence, always the designated "other."[15]

What seems to be pessimism is based on the reality of having to deal with racism from whites for so long. Whenever black people affirm their humanity, white people are threatened. White people seem unable to tolerate the affirmation of the humanity of black people and others classified as non-white—thus the tendency towards separatism remains strong.

As difficult as the first two options are, a third one is even more difficult. This option is to seek to engage white people and white society with dignity. It is the most difficult option because it requires delicate balancing, reading nuances in foreign territory, and constant wariness—an inability to relax except on rare occasions. It often means being seen as militant by whites and as being a sell-out by one's own culture. Yet it may be the only hope for all of us as a society. The engagement of white people by those classified as non-white may be our only hope of extricating ourselves from the disastrous system of race.

It is a perilous journey, and those of us who claim the name "white" are asked to understand the peril but also to see this engagement as a gift, as a glimpse of hope in a deteriorating world. Inez Giles, one of our black elders, offers an interpretation of this journey. She and Nibs have often done workshops together on racism:

In one particular workshop when the white folks were particularly rowdy, Nibs answered one person with these words: "Instead of attacking Inez, we should be grateful to her for letting white people glimpse her life as a black person. On many levels, she is an idiot for fooling with white folks." Instead of comforting me, his words stung me. Here I was being attacked, and my pastor and my friend was calling me an idiot. So much for pastoral concern!

Yet, as I thought about it later, I decided that he was right. I am an idiot for fooling with white folks. It causes nothing but trouble, and in a world of troubles, who needs more? So, I find my life vacillating between the need for shelter and haven of my people and the call I feel to work against racism. To work against racism means to fool with white folks. And that ain't no fun! They deny my feelings; they are offended by me; they offend me; they deny my humanity. Who needs it?

As strange as it may seem for a person to admit to being an idiot for any reason, I must say that it is true. After asking myself many times, Why am I putting myself through all of this turmoil? The answer has become very clear. I am an idiot for fooling with white folks. As I wonder what to do with these feelings, I recall that St. Paul mentioned the foolishness of God. So, I guess you could say that I am a fool for Christ! I am speaking as a black female. I do not claim to speak for all black people, but I do believe that my story reflects a general sense of what it means to be black in this country.

I am an African-American woman, born and reared in the South prior to and during the civil rights movement. I am also an elder in the multiracial Oakhurst Presbyterian Church in Decatur, Georgia; and my pastor is a white man. It should be no surprise that these two parts of myself have not often fit well together. The whole purpose of the system of race is to make certain that whites and blacks do not get together as equals and as partners.[16]

Inez reminds us of the cost of this third option for people classified as nonwhite. To engage white folks as equals is difficult. It requires great dexterity. Nibs was reminded of this journey recently in a workshop on leadership for a local county. A black attorney working in a predominantly white law firm expressed the difficulty of trying to affirm his African heritage while being aware that such an affirmation would be seen as offensive by many of the whites. He spoke of the internal debate in his own soul as he sought to steer a course toward being offered a partnership while still affirming his heritage.

These are the reasons for the great divide, for the lack of enthusiasm for embracing the diversity that God has created as a gift. Yet we must embrace it as a gift if we are to survive and grow as a people.

The Task Force to Combat Racism of the Presbytery of Greater Atlanta has developed a list of steps for moving towards affirming diversity as a gift. The task force was started by Gayraud Wilmore, retired Presbyterian professor and author, and Nibs, and the steps that are shared here can be applied in any situation, most especially local churches. Here are the steps:

1. White folks must come out of denial. Most white folks often deny that they participate in the system of race, and their denial only strengthens the power of race in their lives and in the lives of others. Some white folks are more open about their participation in the system of race, but some are not conscious of it. The first step to healing is a recognition of this participation.

2. White folks are asked to consider the gifts that await them by affirming diversity as an opportunity rather than seeing it as a problem. White folks can regain the humanity that has been lost to them if they begin to affirm diversity. All of us, then, are asked to see the "other" as human beings like us and are asked to see humanity as a circle or a family rather than as a ladder or a hierarchy.

3. Hispanic (Latino) folks, African-American folks, Asian folks, Native American folks, and all others classified as "nonwhite" are asked to acknowledge how difficult it is to live in the system of race—there is often pain, self-hate, anger, and struggle.

4. These same folks are asked to hold on to what has enabled their ancestors to survive in this system—a whole different definition of their humanity, the power of community, the celebration of their lives and culture.

5. These same folks are asked to "come out," to engage white folks as human beings. It is recognized that such encounters in the past have

resulted in imprisonment, torture, and execution. This is the first generation in U.S. history where such "coming out" is not immediately and
universally life threatening.

6. We are all asked to have an active encounter with someone in the
    "other" racial category on *the issue of race*.
7. We are all asked to continue to participate in ongoing workshops to
    combat racism and to affirm diversity.
8. We are all asked to have continuing engagement spiritually on individ-
    ual and community levels with the power of racism. For individuals,
    prayer or meditation, readings, conscious development are necessary
    steps. There are numerous areas in the community where engagement
    is possible—schools, neighborhoods, places of worship, criminal jus-
    tice, economic development, employment, etc. At all levels, remember
    how slippery and how powerful is the system of race.[17]

These are difficult steps to hear and to acknowledge. While here is not the
venue to flesh them out, we do want to emphasize their usefulness in helping
us all to confront and to begin to overcome the power of race that resides in
our hearts and in our institutions.[18] The issue of white denial is fundamental.
It is the central barrier to the affirmation of diversity, for few of us who are
classified as white will admit that racism has captured our hearts and our
modes of perceiving the realities of the world. Nibs experienced this denial in
his own heart in a conversation early in our ministry at Oakhurst. A black
member called to tell him that she had a concern about an area of his leadership. As they continued to talk, Nibs asked her, "Why are you so angry about
this?" She replied, "I'm not angry. What makes you think that I'm angry?"
"Well, you sounded angry," Nibs answered. "No, I'm not angry. If I was
angry, believe me, you would know it—there would be no room for doubt.
Now, tell me again—why do you think I'm angry?" "Well, I'm not sure—you
just sounded angry to me," said Nibs. "No, I'm not angry—but I can tell you
why you asked me why I was angry," she replied. "Why is that?" Nibs asked.
"Because you are not accustomed to black people calling you into question.
So, instead of admitting that, you tried to put the problem onto me by accus-
ing me of being angry, when all the time it was you. That's the problem with
many white folks. Ya'll aren't used to dealing with us as peers. Am I right?"
    There was a long silence as Nibs tried to process her words and as he wres-
tled with how to respond. Was it true? Was his racism showing? And, if it
was true, how should he respond? Should he deny it? Should he acknowledge it? How much would it cost him to acknowledge it? After he wrestled
for what seemed to him to be an eternity, he finally spoke, "I think you might
be right. I don't have much practice with black folks as peers. I'm accus-

tomed to being the authority. I've got a lot to learn." To his surprise, the church member thanked him for his honesty, thanked him for not denying the obvious racism and the transparent attempt to shift responsibility for it to her. It was one of many fundamental turning points for us in the ministry at Oakhurst, on at least two levels. On one level, Nibs's racism had been exposed to the church member—he had not been able to hide it from her. He learned in this conversation that white folks cannot hide our racism from those we classify as nonwhite. It is plain to see, and Nibs was only fooling himself to think that he had hidden it from her. On another level, Nibs's racism had been exposed *to him*—and this is the most important level. When exposed, he chose—through God's grace—not to flee, not to seek denial, but to acknowledge it. He was able to take a tiny step of acknowledgement, and it has made a fundamental difference.

Another example stresses this same point. During the last fifteen years at Oakhurst, we have noticed that many of the white families leave the church when their children reach school age. For some, it seemed to be coincidence; for others, there seemed to be a pattern. At one of our forums when we turned to public education, one of our white members in their early fifties made a revelation that startled many. She had just joined Oakhurst and, in this discussion, revealed that she had wanted to become involved here several years earlier. She stated that she deliberately chose to wait, however, until her children finished high school so that they would not have to encounter black youth in their church setting. During those years, she stayed in her white church. It was a painful revelation, but no black person in the audience was surprised. They know only too well how much white parents fear their children's encounters with black children. Instead of castigating our new member, though, they thanked her for her honesty. They gave thanks that at least one white person admitted that race played a part in her decision making. Rather than denying that race was powerful in her life, this member admitted how important it was to her, and in so doing, opened up her heart and the hearts of many others for a dialogue and an encounter.

Another step that needs to be lifted up is that we ask people classified as nonwhite, as "colored," to "come out," to use the language of the gay and lesbian liberation movement. In this sense, we ask those classified as "other" to engage white folks as human beings, to engage white folks as peers. Such engagement might seem obvious until we consider that this generation is the first in which nonwhite people could act like real people in the presence of white people. In previous generations, to do so would be to risk violence, arrest, and even death. So it is a fearful prospect, but these kinds of encounters are essential if we are to begin to overcome the power of racism.

Another story should clear up any fuzziness. Several years ago, a black grandmother who was a member of Oakhurst called to tell Nibs that she would have to take her granddaughter out of the church. This young girl, who was five years old at the time, had attended Oakhurst all of her life. The grandmother told Nibs that she thought that her granddaughter was getting too comfortable around white people. She had learned to be comfortable at Oakhurst, where, for the most part, people had tried to treat her as a child of God. When Nibs asked the grandmother why she needed to take her out of Oakhurst, she gave an example. One day she and her granddaughter were in a mall when a white man bumped into the granddaughter and kept on walking, without stopping to apologize. The granddaughter turned to the man and said, "You forgot to say excuse me." The white man paid no attention and kept walking. The little girl ran after him, got his attention, then said again, "You forgot to say excuse me." The man then apologized.

The grandmother told this story as an example of what had happened to her granddaughter at Oakhurst. She had encountered white people as human beings, and they had treated her as a human being. Because of this experience, she expected all white people to receive her as a human being. She had lost sight of the system of race, and this "color blindness" was dangerous. Such an expectation could get her hurt or killed. Nibs was reminded of the terrible dilemma in which those classified as nonwhite find themselves: deny your humanity out in the white world or risk great hurt. As the grandmother discussed this situation with Nibs, it became clear that the little girl had "come out," had affirmed her humanity in a white world, choosing not to shrink back or be cautious. She had chosen rather to act like a person.

As the discussion continued, Nibs began to understand that the decision for nonwhite people is not whether to avoid the hurt, for they have little choice. The system of race will hurt those classified as nonwhite—there is little doubt about that. That is the purpose of the system of race. The decision for nonwhite people is how to receive and appropriate the pain. The grandmother and Nibs both agreed that it was preferable for the granddaughter to be hurt by her strength rather than giving in to the system of race and turning the process inward and accepting the white definition of herself. To come out, to affirm her humanity in the white world would surely lead to hurt and rebuttal by that white world. To deny her humanity in the white world, though, would lead to a deeper hurt that allowed white people to define her. The question was not how to avoid the pain but rather how to prepare for it and use it as an instrument of growth and resistance rather than as a vehicle to self-destruction. It was agreed that the granddaughter should stay at Oakhurst and keep practicing her coming out. It was also agreed that such coming out would also act as a catalyst for white people to encounter their own racism by encountering their own feelings and reactions when nonwhite people refuse to accept the idea of white superiority.

Since this is not a book on race, we will not go into further details about the steps that are listed. We must note, however, that these steps describe an ongoing process that seeks to help us all loosen the power of racism in our hearts and to help us affirm the power and possibilities of diversity. Seeing diversity as a gift and as a hope are fundamental to the development of multicultural ministry. In this chapter, we have sought to outline the main obstacles that prevent people in our culture from affirming diversity. The racism that we have learned and have accepted prevents us from believing that those classified as "other" not only are not a threat to us but rather have great gifts to offer us. This stubbornness on race is especially true for those classified as white, who see ourselves at the top of the racial ladder.

This journey of coming to understand the power of race and how it has captured our hearts has had an unexpected benefit. It has opened up the world of biblical language and biblical realities for us at Oakhurst in a new way. As we indicated in chapter 2, the struggle with racism in our own hearts and in our institutions has caused us to gain insight into the strange biblical language of demons, powers, and principalities. As modern folk and even "postmodern" folk, we have had difficulty discerning the meaning of biblical language that often seems primitive and unsophisticated. Our struggles with racism have helped us reclaim the meaning and the insights of this language.

When Paul writes something like "You were dead through your trespasses and sins in which you once lived, following the course of this world, following the ruler of the power of the air. . . ." (Eph. 2:1), what in the world is he talking about? Who is the "ruler of the power of the air"? Many of us have trouble grasping the meaning of that phrase because we have ceased to believe in a "ruler of the air," a power that hovers over us and in us, waiting to capture us. Paul's point seems hopelessly lost because it centers on a concept that seems completely outdated and thus empty of meaning for us in the twenty-first century.

If we examine this concept a bit, however, and consider its meaning in the context of the continuing power of something like racism, then the reality to which it points can be comprehended. The "power of the air" is that which enables all of us to breathe and to live. Without the power of the air, none of us would be alive to contemplate the meaning of such a phrase. In this sense, the power of the air is that which gives us life. In using a phrase like "ruler of the power of the air," then, Paul is indicating that the very structures that give us life have been taken over by powers that use these life-giving structures to lead us to death.

In this sense, Paul emphasizes that the structures of life have been captured by death. Our becoming "dead through trespasses and sins" is not so much a matter of our weak wills being taken over by a tyrannical or seductive power, though that is certainly part of the process. It is actually a matter that is much more threatening and radical. Our becoming dead is a matter of life-giving structures leading us to death. Like the very air that we breathe that gives us life, these structures begin to capture our hearts and our imaginations before we have any idea that they are doing it. The power of racism comes not only from mean-spirited people who clearly want to dominate and to crush others but from decent people accepting its premises and teaching it to others, all of whom live as if the power of race is ultimate.

As we indicated in chapter 2, we who are white were taught racism as children, long before we knew that we were receiving it. Our learning racism was not a matter of the will—it was taught to us long before we had any idea that we could reject it. By the time we discovered how deadly it was to us and to others, it had already intertwined itself with our self-definitions and thus has become exceedingly difficult to remove. Like the "power of the air," it was taught to us by "good" people, by our families, by our churches, by our teachers. Those who loved us and nurtured us and who taught us to love also taught us racism. This description is not a rejection of our past, revealing how terrible our parents and churches were. Indeed, we give thanks to God for our parents and teachers every day, and for our churches, where we experienced in profound ways the loving presence of God. This description is rather a revelation of the radical nature of sinfulness, the nature that Paul describes in the beginning of Eph. 2. The people and the institutions who gave us life—"the power of the air"—also taught us racism.

Rather than indicting our forebears, this discussion recognizes how the power of sinfulness works. It is our opening into the meaning and power of the biblical language. It recognizes that we have taught and are teaching our children some of these same sinful structures, even as we love them and nurture them. We have taught them in this manner not because we are mean and evil but because, like our forebears, anxiety and fear and idolatry have captured our hearts, too. The ruler of the power of the air has captured us also. Our children and grandchildren will look back on us with a keener eye than we have, and we hope that they are able to discern the places where we helped make them captives to the "ruler" of the air. This does not mean that the structures of life are corrupt at their core—it rather means that they, too, have been captured by the power of domination. How that captivity came about is as old as the question of the origin of evil, but our point is that the depth of the power of sinfulness—a depth described in biblical language but often lost to us twenty centuries later—is much deeper and more radical than many of us had previously thought. The struggle over racism has helped us to recapture the power and depth of the biblical language.

Two years ago, Nibs was teaching a course on racism at Columbia Seminary. He asked the students to name some areas in which they had experienced the power of race. One of the young white women students noted that when her parents had helped her move into the seminary two years earlier, her mother had cautioned her not to shop at a grocery store nearby because the vast majority of customers were black. The student took this warning as a blatant sign of racism, which she was dismayed to experience so bluntly and so clearly in her mother. As we discussed this encounter, it served as a portal into the biblical realities concerning sinfulness. The mother was not being mean-spirited in cautioning her daughter. Rather, she was trying to protect her daughter and keep her safe. The mother had come to believe that black people are dangerous, especially to young white women, and she was acting in a protective capacity with her daughter, as any decent parent would. While the mother's intent may not have been mean-spirited, the results were. In her acceptance of the power of racism and in her using that acceptance to caution her daughter, she perpetuated racism's power to dehumanize a whole set of people without regard to their individual character. She did this not out of a desire to hurt black people but to protect her daughter, just as she would caution her not to swim alone or play out in the street. The very act of seeking to protect her daughter had let her into the labyrinth of the sin of racism.

The biblical witness concerning this situation is that the mother was possessed by the demonic power of racism. This idea of demonic possession is not the head-twisting, venom-spewing kind. It rather describes a spiritual force that takes over the perceptual apparatus and, at times, the personality of people who have been taught and who have accepted the power of racism. This spiritual force transformed a loving mother who, in seeking to protect her own daughter, dismissed the humanity of many other daughters and sons. It is the reality described by the biblical language of demonic possession. While demonic possession may not make faces contort or cause heads to spin round and round, it does cause a decent Presbyterian elder to "redline" neighborhoods in order that a subsidiary of her bank can charge excessive interest rates on loans made in that neighborhood, thus participating in predatory lending practices.[19] While demonic possession may not cause violent shaking of the body, it does cause parents to teach their children racism in the name of protecting those same children.

In this way, Paul's language in Ephesians about being "dead through your trespasses and sins" (2:1) comes alive, so to speak. Through the power of racism, we have become dead to ourselves and to others in refusing to consider their humanity and our own humanity. Because of this demonic possession by the power of racism, we find it difficult to believe in the life-sustaining gifts of diversity—indeed, we cannot even imagine them. It is a depressing scenario, but the promise of the gospel is that we are not hopelessly lost in the quagmire of racism or any of the other powers that seek to define us. As Paul emphasizes throughout his body of letters in the New Testament, God's grace brings us life and hope and possibility. The radical nature of the grace of God enables us to find new life. Paul emphasizes this concept several times in the first ten verses of Ephesians 2: "by grace you have been saved." In this sense, grace doesn't make us good or righteous. Rather, it opens up possibilities in our hearts, offering us the opportunity to see a whole new reality, a whole new way of life. Our imaginations—so captured by the powers that we cannot even comprehend another possibility—are offered a new vision through the grace of God. As Jesus puts it in John 10:10: "I have come that they may have life, and have it more abundant than they ever imagined" (paraphrase).

The remainder of the second chapter of Ephesians is an unfolding of the meaning of this new life in relation to racism. Where once we were dead in our trespasses and sins, now through grace we have been saved. Where once we were strangers and aliens, now we are one new humanity, citizens and members of the household of God. Paul lifts up the cross as the locus of this transformation:

> But now in Christ Jesus you who once were far off have been brought near by the blood of Christ. For he is our peace; in his flesh he has made both groups into one and has broken down the dividing wall, that is, the hostility between us. He has abolished the law with its commandments and ordinances, that he might create in himself one new humanity in place of the two, thus making peace, and might reconcile both groups to God in one body through the cross, thus putting to death that hostility through it. So he came and proclaimed peace to you who were far off and peace to those who were near. (2:13–17)

The image of the cross of Jesus Christ reveals to us the cost and the depth of our captivity to the "ruler of the power of the air," but the cross also proclaims the victory of God over the ruler of the air, thus offering us and all of creation a new possibility. Rather than seeing one another as enemies, as aliens and strangers, we now have the possibility of seeing one another and experiencing one another as sisters and brothers, members of the family of God.

The struggle with racism and how it diminishes our capacity to see diversity as a gift is an entry point into biblical language and the realities that it describes.

It is not the only entry point into the biblical world, however, for there are unfortunately many others, including materialism and gender issues. This journey enables us to gain a glimpse of our radical captivity to the power of sinfulness. Only when we see the biblical realities in this way can we begin to comprehend the great gift that is ours in the grace of the God we know in Jesus Christ. This grace offers us new life, new vision, new hope, new possibility—living not as strangers and aliens but as citizens and members of the household of God. We have seen a glimpse of that vision in our life together at Oakhurst. The remainder of this book will be a description of how we seek at Oakhurst to live in that new vision, all the while recognizing that the struggles will remain because we continue to carry in our hearts and in our minds the residue of the ruler of the power of the air.

Chapter Four

Life Together: How We Worship and Learn

Oakhurst, which has a congregation that is roughly half black and half white, is what diversity is all about: people of different races coming together not in the mournful, candle-bearing aftermath of some urban riot or the artificially arranged precursor to some political photo op, but because they want *to be together. Things in America tend toward being all one thing or all the other. Schools, parties, circles of friends, television sitcoms are often mostly or entirely white or mostly or entirely black. It's especially rare to see a church that is racially mixed with such equanimity.*

*T*his quote from *Time Magazine*[1] moves to the heart of our life together as diverse people: we want to be together. Many of us come to Oakhurst out of a sense that we should be there: we ought to be part of such a community. Some of us come out of fascination, as if seeing an exotic flower or animal: Can such a being really exist? Some of us come out of a sense of longing: Can this be the place where our restless hearts will gain a glimpse of home? Some of us come out of hopefulness that fights against despair: Is there really hope for the church to be a place where spirituality and social justice are woven together without one overwhelming the other? Whatever people's initial motives are for coming to Oakhurst, they will not stay unless they decide that it is a place where they desire to be. Our life together breaks too many molds and calls for too much self-examination for anyone to stay long without a desire to do so. Our coming together and staying together, then, is a continuing education process. We will always be educating those who come to us concerning the powers that have defined them and concerning the possibility of new life. We who are veterans of Oakhurst will continue to be educated as God brings new people, new perspectives, and new possibilities.

All of this process begins in worship. Worship is our central act as a community of faith. Even in this beginning point, we as pastors have been reeducated and continue to be. We came of age in the 1960s, an era that called everything into question, including and especially the church and its worship. While some of the questioning was likely akin to adolescent rebellion, much was necessary and on target. As was asked in chapter 1, what kind of church is it that excludes people from its worship solely on the basis of their racial classification? In that kind of atmosphere, the questioning of the church and its worship can be seen as the Holy Spirit knocking on the door.

We were part of that questioning, and we saw worship in churches that were exclusive and repressive and irrelevant and more interested in preserving the social and economic status of their members than in being the body of Christ. We came to believe, as many did, that the importance of worship should be diminished in favor of the strengthening of social justice and community ministry. For us, worship was a necessary act that pointed towards real ministry: justice and service to others. As we began to lead worship on a regular basis in Norfolk and Nashville as pastors, we shifted a bit, but clearly the importance of worship was secondary to justice and service.

Then we came to Oakhurst and encountered a whole different worship tradition. Here we encountered not the regular Presbyterian tradition that often blessed the middle and upper classes, but rather the African American tradition which saw worship as life-giving and life-sustaining. Here we encountered the concept that one might actually engage the living presence of God in worship rather than the concept of a God who was grateful for getting an hour a week of our time in a busy schedule. Here we found people who knew that when they stepped outside the church doors, they would immediately be dehumanized as black people, as consumers, as women. Here we found people who came to worship God not as an afterthought and not out of "oughtness," but because they had to come in order to find life—their lives depended on worship. In the world, they heard and experienced that they were nobody. In worship, they heard and experienced that they were somebody, that they were children of God. They came to worship as thirsty people come to water. They came to worship to hear their true definitions as daughters and sons of God. Not perfect by any means but claimed as children in the life, death, and resurrection of Jesus Christ.

Our previous understanding of worship, then, was completely turned around. Here at Oakhurst we learned that worship was not an exercise in assuring ourselves that God had blessed us. Here at Oakhurst we learned that worship was a life-sustaining, life-changing, celebrating, challenging act of praise and thanksgiving. We were startled, and we were astonished to find ourselves agreeing with the long and deep Christian tradition that worship is our central act together. Rather than seeing worship as antagonistic to justice and service as we had experienced in the 1960s, we began to see it as the blood that runs through the vessels of justice and service. We began to see worship as that which enabled us to find our true center and our true definition so that we would be able to seek justice and serve others over the long haul. If there is no work for justice and service to others, there are gaping holes in the body, and the blood runs out or dries up and loses its vitality. If there is no vital worship, there are no nutrients to sustain the justice and service, and the body hardens and dies.

We received this great gift of worship at Oakhurst and have tried to build on its powerful foundation by weaving several themes into its fabric: The first is celebration and thanksgiving. We come not as long-faced, repressed folks who feel that they must be grumpy while worshiping God. We come rather as those who celebrate God's love in our lives and who give thanks to God for the power of life, even in the midst of the power of death. At the heart of our worship is celebration and thanksgiving: "If the only prayer you say in your entire life is 'Thank You!' that would suffice," said Meister Eckhart.[2] We give thanks to God for claiming us and defining us. We give thanks to God for redeeming us. We give thanks to God for sustaining us.

Because we seek to be open to the leading of God's Spirit in this celebration and praise, our worship often seems to be structured chaos. We have the same form each Sunday, but the content is rarely ever the same. We have two adult choirs and our children's choir, with various musicians from the congregation lending a hand on occasion. Sometimes there will be shouts of "Hallelujah! Thank You, Jesus!" Sometimes there will be clapping; sometimes there will be African drummers; sometimes someone will step out in a liturgical dance. There is a sense in which the unexpected is almost expected and a sense in which the Spirit of God is moving, with an emphasis on the gifts that God wants to bestow upon us.

These emphases on celebration and thanksgiving and newness strengthen us to confront the powers in ourselves and out in the world. We emphasize each Sunday that the powers are inside us, seeking to capture our hearts so that we will worship them. We are aware that the power of death seeks us out to convince us that it is ultimate. In worship at Oakhurst, we seek to affirm the ultimate, life-giving power of God and to acknowledge how much we resist that life-giving power because our hearts have surrendered to other powers. As on the occasion described below, we hear and experience this proclamation:

They stand in front of the curtain in the fellowship hall of Oakhurst Presbyterian Church on a Sunday morning. On cue, they begin singing at our Sunday school kick-off rally. They dance, roll their arms, and giggle as they sing "Jesus is the rock who rolls my blues away," a song they learned together at church camp the previous summer. We have nicknamed them the "Supremes" after the famous 1960s singing group. Their names are Noelle, a fifth grader whose parents were born in Jamaica; Tiffany, a sixth grader whose parents are African-American; and my daughter, Susan, a sixth grader of European ancestry. They are part of the vision and hope of Oakhurst.

On another occasion, the sanctuary is filled to overflowing. It is a sad and mournful time, the funeral of a young African-American woman who died of a rare blood disease. She was an outstanding teacher and left behind a teen-age son at her death. Two women, one white and one black, sing together of sorrow and thanksgiving for the life and work of our departed sister, taken so early from us. At the close of the service, a lone dancer steps forward, a young African-American woman who had been a student of the sister who passed. Dressed all in black, she dances to the song "To Be Young, Gifted, and Black"; and as she moves across the front of the sanctuary, she addresses the coffin. She doesn't plead with the coffin—she slaps it! She slaps it to express our anger at the loss. She slaps it to give thanks for the life of our sister. She slaps it to tell death that there is a "great getting' up morning," to tell death that its power is not final or domineering. The gift of life and the gift of love that we know through God is the center of all that exists.[3]

In seeking to weave these themes together, we concentrated on seven elements of worship that helped us all to shift towards these themes: Our time of greeting, the sharing of concerns and joys, the sermon, the music, the sacraments, our approach to art, and Christian education.

Greeting Time

The first element was the greeting of the people described in chapter 2, in which there is much more than turning around to shake the hand of someone in the next pew. In our greeting time, people, including children and youth, move all over the sanctuary to shake hands, hug, and generally create a new space in the sanctuary and inside ourselves, making room for the movement of the Spirit. This greeting can continue for seven to ten minutes, and we are called back to our seats with the playing of the organ.

Sharing of Concerns and Joys

A second element that was added was called sharing of concerns and joys, followed by a pastoral prayer seeking to weave them all together. On many

Sundays, people are encouraged to stand up and verbally share joys or concerns for prayers. This ritual affirms unity and commonality in our diversity—everyone knows sickness and frailty; everyone has experienced sorrows; everyone has experienced moments of joy. We had done this in a smaller church in Norfolk and had seen its power to break down barriers and to build the community. In our whiteness, we did not realize what we were asking of black people in this ritual. One of our black members came to us soon after this ritual was used in worship and expressed concern that we were asking too much of our black members. They pointed out that black people had survived for centuries by keeping white people out of their lives as much as possible. And now we were creating pressure and asking black people to share their lives in the midst of white people. We expressed our gratitude to this member for raising this issue and for reminding us how little we knew about black life. Yet we also emphasized that we would continue the ritual for a bit longer to see what developed.

Our sharing time has proved to be one of our most powerful tools for building community among diverse people and for gaining new members. We have discovered a longing in the hearts of many to be known, to be known in their fragility and vulnerability, to be able to share their longings and fears in safe space. And the space has become safe for our African American members, a place in worship where hopes and fears can be acknowledged. It is a ritual in which we affirm the frailty, the humanity, and the possibility of our lives. It is a time when our true definitions are made clear as children of God: we are dependent on God and on one another, counting on God's grace and God's movement in our lives to redeem us and sustain us. It has been a powerful vehicle for discovering that God truly has broken down the dividing walls. Chuck Foster and Ted Brelsford described it like this:

> Similar risks are taken in Sunday worship. A feeling of Presbyterian decency and order sets the tone for the service. Within that structural framework congregants also have experiences of "anti-structure." About midway in the service Nibs leaves the chancel to march up the middle aisle toward the center of the sanctuary, where he stands midway between the stained-glass windows with the dark and light images of Jesus. There he invites congregants to share joys and concerns. Anyone may stand and say whatever he or she wants—for as long as he or she wants. Some do not just say it. One elderly African-American woman occasionally moves to the center aisle and Nibs slowly takes a seat while she sings her witness—a soulful solo on the joys or burden (or both) of life and faith. Most of the joys and concerns are personal and fairly brief, though details are considered important. . . . Even those who complain seem not to question Nibs's right to let it "go on." Nibs admits he is sometimes uncomfortable when too many

sharings are long. But he takes it all in stride, affirming and reiterating and contextualizing whatever comes.

Nibs has an astounding memory. He can weave fifteen or twenty joys and concerns into an all-inclusive pastoral prayer—without notes. But it is the contextualizing of each prayer request that is so powerful and so pedagogically significant. Immediately after a concern is shared Nibs repeats the concern for the rest of the congregation, points out its theological or social significance, and sometimes relates it to other concerns of the congregation. After all have shared, he groups the sharings around theological and social themes in his pastoral prayer, framing everything in terms of human sinfulness and divine grace. It becomes clear when Nibs leads the congregation in prayer that, for these folk, God is active in this world and the details of their lives are all ultimately meaningful and important.[4]

The two elements of greeting and sharing concerns and joys have been great gifts in developing our multicultural community of faith, but they have not come without pain or controversy. Their combined length can sometimes be thirty to forty minutes, and if the time allowed for worship is only sixty minutes, then there are obviously problems. The biggest hurdle in this area was the expectation of a sixty-minute limit on worship. When we consistently took longer than sixty minutes for worship, the complaints grew. We began to have major battles in our elders's meetings about this issue. On one particular Sunday when we were celebrating the sacrament of the Lord's supper, we did not begin the sacrament until 1 p.m. One elder commented that they were so hostile when they came to the sacrament that they were in no mood to receive it—they pointed out that this did not seem to be a good foundation for participating in the sacrament. Another elder, a charter member of the church, stopped coming to worship. When they were asked why they stopped coming, their reply was, "What they do now at Oakhurst is not worship."

Balanced against this tide of criticism and complaints were the testimonies of the new members who began to join. In Presbyterian churches, those people wishing to join as members are required to meet with the group of elders known as the session. Almost all of those who joined in this early period of establishing new rituals testified that one of the things that attracted them to Oakhurst was this sharing of concerns and joys. Here is the testimony of one such member:

The Sharing of Joys and Concerns at Oakhurst is truly a time of POWER-FUL fellowship and prayer. It is a time when people from all walks of life can come together as a community and share in their pain and their fears; their joy and celebrations.

It is a time when a woman can stand up and ask for prayers as she goes through chemotherapy for breast cancer. It is a time when another can stand up and share her concerns for the neighborhood and for her children. It is a time when a man can stand and ask that we remember the people of Yugoslavia. It is a time when a mother can stand and tell about her son's successful athletic team and how proud she is of him. It is a time when a young child can stand up and ask for prayers for his father. It is a time when the congregation can cry together over the death of one of their members. It is a time when the congregation can rejoice together in the birth of a new baby.[5]

We sought to work out a compromise because of the strong feelings on each side. Some of the veteran white members began formally to leave the church or quietly to stop coming. Yet we were also beginning to receive many younger members, both black and white. We established that the time allotted for worship was established by God's Spirit, not by the human clock. We acknowledged that we would seek to cut down on what seemed to be announcements during the sharing time. We normally celebrate the sacrament of the Lord's Supper on the first Sunday of each month, and we decided that, on those Sundays, the concerns and joys would be written down on sheets of paper to be given to the pastors and read by them at the sharing time. The pastors agreed to begin to signal people to bring their sharing to a close if it was going on a bit long. As our congregation has grown, we have used the papers more often because there are simply so many more people in worship. It is not uncommon to have twenty to thirty people share concerns and joys.

This decision to turn the time and space of worship over to God's Spirit has had an extraordinary effect on all of us. Worship has once again regained its traditional vitality as the center of our lives together. It has helped us all to frame in our hearts and in our minds the truth that our lives and indeed all of life belong to God. Nothing emphasizes that more in worship than not knowing quite when it will end or what will be the specific content of worship. In this way, we seek to emphasize the importance and the validity of God's Spirit moving in our worship, moving to shake us up, to take us up, to help us find our true home as children of God.

The Sermon

A third element—the sermon—was not added by us because, as in any good Presbyterian church with the emphasis on the Word of God, the sermon is a central part of worship. While we did not need to establish its importance in a Presbyterian congregation, we did tinker with it a bit. When we came to Oakhurst, the sermon was at the end of the worship service. We had learned in seminary that Reformed theology emphasizes that the sermon should be towards the center of worship, emphasizing the response of the people to the Word preached. This time of response can include the offering, prayers of the people or pastoral prayer, special occasions, affirmations of faith, and hymns. We discussed this approach with the worship committee at Oakhurst, and they saw its wisdom, especially since we had been to seminary! The sermon was moved from the end of the service toward the center, and we felt that all was right in the reformation of Oakhurst.

After a couple of months, however, several African American members met with us to voice their concerns about our having moved the sermon. They emphasized that in the African American tradition, the sermon was at the end, the climax of the worship service. We explained that the object of the Reformed mode with the sermon at the center of worship, was to provide an opportunity for the response of the people. We emphasized that this response was the main point of the sermon, and we pointed out the various elements of our worship that offered time for such a response. They, however, hoped that we would see it in a different way and suggested that rather than viewing the response of the people as the ten to fifteen minutes after the sermon, we should view the response of the people as what they did for the rest of the week—what they did when they went out the doors of the sanctuary. Their approach hit home—the response of the people to the sermon was to be what they did with their lives rather than what we did at the end of worship. We saw the wisdom of their approach, and we moved the sermon back to the end of worship, where it still stands.

We have also tried to use the sermon as a time of teaching, a time of opening up the biblical texts, and a time of bringing together the power and the truth of the tradition to bear on our contemporary lives. Our purpose is not so much to make the sermons relevant as it is to make them real and to help the biblical text come alive. We have used a variety of methods, such as dialogue sermons between the two of us, as well as trialogue sermons with our pastoral assistant or student intern. We have sometimes used a dramatic presentation where one of us becomes a character in the biblical story and the sermon is presented from that character's point of view. Nibs sometimes sings in his sermons, which is good for a laugh and always wakes people up! Though we have not adopted the black preaching style of whooping and hollering, we have adopted that tradition's belief that the personality of the preacher is part of the sermon and that conviction and drama and even pounding the pulpit have their place.

Some traditions teach that the personality of the preacher is to be laid aside so that the objective truth of the Bible can be preached. We have learned over our thirty years of preaching that the personality of the preacher is never laid aside. At best, we can repress it a bit, but it will always make itself known in the sermon. In this sense, the point of the sermon is not to get rid of the vessel but to let the message be mediated through the life and personality of the preacher. There is, of course, great danger in this approach, because the personality and the beliefs of the preacher can often overwhelm or cloud the biblical text. The balancing point is to center the sermon on the biblical text. Often the sermons that we preach are dialogues between the text and our own lives and struggles.

In our preaching we use many stories and illustrations, and we try to make certain that every sermon serves as a bridge between the text and the congregation. Yet we try not to allow our stories or the bridge building to dominate the text. In the biblical passages from our sacred texts we meet the Spirit of God. We try to be provocative and evocative in our approach to the texts and the sermons based on them. We try to provoke all of us out of our doldrums with the Bible in order to encounter the richness and power of the sacred texts. We try to evoke or call out God's Spirit to speak to each and all of us so that all worshiping with us will find a place in the biblical story where they meet themselves and meet God. Our method is to begin our sermon preparation in our own journeys. Where does the text speak to us? Where does it grab us or provoke us or excite us or disturb us? We seek to balance this personal grounding with the necessary scholarly work, all with an ear and an eye for the power of the text in our world today and in our particular community of faith. The purpose of our sermons is not so much to tell people what the biblical texts mean as to open up their power for the congregation so that God's Spirit may move into all of our lives. In our preaching, we seek to honor the Bible not as a book that tells us what to do but as a book that tells us who God is and who we are.

Music

A fourth element on which we focused was music in worship, perhaps the most powerful and most moving and most controversial of all the elements of worship. We have already related in chapter 2 the struggle over hiring one of our choir directors. After that particular choir director left, we began a difficult search for a replacement. There were two major obstacles. The first was lack of funding—we were way below the market level in what we could afford to pay. Whoever came to direct our choir would have to do it as a calling. The second obstacle was the same one that we had faced previously—Would this choir director be black or white? What kind of music would he or she direct? These obstacles joined with the revelation that some of our African American youth were beginning to sing in the youth choirs in other churches. Our session decided at that point to seek a solution that many other churches had used: we would have two choirs. One choir would be our regular "European" choir, the choir that we had at that point. A second choir would be started, a choir that would be oriented towards black youth and black gospel music. The European choir was renamed the Chancel Choir, and the second choir was named the Sanctuary Mass Choir, under the direction of Joann Price, who came to us in 1989.

Both choirs fill needs and desires in our congregation, but it is the Mass Choir that elicits the most passionate responses—from clapping to shouting to praising. After the Mass Choir began and the responses to its music began, people were not certain how to respond to the music of the Chancel Choir. Traditionally, the response had been silence in the normal Presbyterian tradition. Gradually, the congregation has begun to occasionally clap in response to the Chancel Choir, sometimes even adding an "Amen!" here and there. The singing styles of the two choirs are in contrast. The Chancel Choir learns its music from written notes on sheets of paper. The Mass Choir learns its music by notes written in the ears and hearts. Some of our members sing in both choirs, and each choir sings twice a month.

The division into two choirs has opened gates for us to appreciate many different kinds of music. From the plaintive notes of the recorder from medieval Europe to the insistent drums of Africa, from guitars in a bluegrass band to the drums and electric guitars of a gospel band—we have heard and continue to hear a wide variety of music. Both of our choirs are integrated, and we've learned that white people can sing gospel music! We have come to appreciate the power of the black singing style, as explained by Bernice Johnson Reagon of Sweet Honey in the Rock:

> Describing Black singing is not easy to put in words. In singing songs in a Black style, you have to be able to change the notes with feelings before the sound comes out of your body. It's like the feelings have to be inside the sound. So you are not singing notes and tones, you are giving out pieces of yourself, coming from places inside that you can only yourself visit in a singing. It is having what is inside yourself ride the air in the song you are singing.[6]

The music ministry of our worship is perhaps its most powerful part. Whereas we as pastors would like to think that the sermons are the most powerful, we know in our hearts the power of music. Each year we have a Gospelfest to raise money for our youth ministry, and it is an exciting, vibrant time where the glory of the Lord is revealed by choirs from all over the city. We have already mentioned the power of the music and the dancer at one of our funerals. At another of our funerals, we had three modes of music—the European style, the gospel style, and a bluegrass band—because the young man who had been tragically killed in a car wreck had sung in both our choirs and had loved playing in a bluegrass band.

The division of our choral music into two choirs was difficult at first, but as the power of the diverse music became clear, the arguments over it have largely evaporated. Rather, we spend that energy in praising God for God's mighty works in our lives and in the life of the world. We have come to believe and to appreciate that there is a variety of musical gifts, and we thank God for opening this rich diversity of music to us.

The Sacraments

The Presbyterian Church recognizes two sacraments: baptism and the Lord's Supper. Our approach to the Lord's Supper has several levels. We emphasize our brokenness and our participation in the injustice and oppression in the world. None of us come to the Lord's Table because we are worthy. We come because our crucified and risen Lord bids us to come, even as we acknowledge that, at this Table, we participate in the execution of Jesus. Almost all of the women and men who gathered with Jesus at the Last Supper deserted him—only a few remained to watch him die and to watch their hopes die with him. We remember that we, too, betray Jesus. That we, too, deny that we even know him; that we, too, flee in terror. Those who gathered with Jesus on that night were just like us.

On another level, however, we remember that, through God's redeeming Spirit, those women and men who seemed to stumble so much became powerful witnesses for Jesus. In the Lord's Supper we give thanks for God's "Yes" to us in the cross, and we claim the grace that God shares with us in the Lord's Supper. On a third level, we emphasize the communal nature of the sacrament. Presbyterian polity greatly discourages "private" sacraments because it is our belief that part of the power of the sacrament comes from its being shared wherever two or three are gathered in His name. In our congregation, this sharing is especially powerful because our body is so diverse. We emphasize in our invitation that everyone who seeks to trust in Jesus, including our children, is welcomed to the Table.

We celebrate the sacrament of the Lord's Supper on the first Sunday of every month and on a few other times. We celebrate the sacrament of baptism whenever the occasion arises. In the sacrament of baptism, we try to emphasize the same levels that we emphasize in the Lord's Supper. We baptize infants because we lift up the grace of God that saves us even before we are aware of who God is. When we baptize an infant, one of us will carry the baby through the center aisle of the sanctuary so that all can see the baby. The point of this stroll is not to show off the infant but to make certain that everyone makes connections, because part of the sacrament of baptism for us at Oakhurst are the vows taken by the congregation to help raise the child. As we walk through the congregation with the baby, we talk about the need for the members of Oakhurst to help the child find his or her true definition as a child of God. If we are baptizing a black baby boy, we emphasize that the world will tell him that he is not worth much, and it will be up to us to help him hear his true definition. If we are baptizing a baby girl, we emphasize that the world will tell her that she should be dominated by men, and it will be up to us to tell her that she is a daughter of God. If we are baptizing a white baby boy, we emphasize that the world will tell him that he should be in control of the world because he is a white male. We ask our congregation to help him find his true definition as a child of God.

In our celebration of the sacrament of baptism, we emphasize the importance of welcoming the baby into our particular church and into the church universal. Because we emphasize the realities that will influence the child's life, this time can turn out to be a powerful moment when we all gain insight into our own status as children of God and into the necessity of proclaiming and living that new reality. One of the mothers of a baby we baptized recently put it this way:

> It's like you're not even in church . . . when Nibs talks, he's talking about stuff outside of the church, about stuff that is relevant in the world. Like with Jemma's baptismal, when he walked around and talked about all the struggles that Jemma would have to face . . . that is going to be real for her, and I appreciated that Nibs spoke about it. . . . I bring Jemma here because she is going to need this support system, being a racially mixed child, with all the problems she will face outside in the world.[7]

Our emphasis is that we are rooted in the gospel and face the powers of the world, both inside us and outside us. As another of our members put it, "I wish that we had a baptism every Sunday—it is where the power of the gospel is emphasized the most and is seen most clearly."

The second chapter of Acts comments that those who came together as the people of God after Pentecost came "with glad and generous hearts" (2:46).

We have that same sense about our life together at Oakhurst, especially our worship. We seek to weave together the realities of the world—our hopes, our fears, our longings, our pain—with the promises and the realities of the God movement in our midst. We try to acknowledge the pain and the difficulties of life and of our particular lives without making people feel guilty for expressing the pain. We try also to acknowledge the glorious freedom of the children of God that has been offered to us in Jesus Christ. We try to encourage a dialogue in our individual hearts and in our community of faith, a dialogue between the hunger and struggles of our lives and the new reality offered by the gospel: no sugarcoating, no repression, but rather expression of passion and longing for God. In this approach, many folk find an honest encounter with God's Holy Spirit, an encounter made most vivid when we close our worship by making a circle in the sanctuary to be led by the Sanctuary Mass Choir in singing "Sweet, Sweet Spirit." As we hold hands and sing and look around at the vast diversity among our congregation, the presence of the Spirit is palpable. In all of this, we seek to orient each and all of us toward the central definition of our lives: we are children of God.

As we have indicated before, not everyone is comfortable with this approach. When we instituted these changes in worship, several white families left, and some who stayed still are grumpy about certain parts of worship. Some, both black and white, groan when the sharing of concerns and joys seems to go too long. Some believe that we are too informal: "There is one thing that I miss. . . . I wish our rituals had more of a sacred tone, more of a sense of awe."[8] Some believe that we emphasize race too much, and some believe that we are too hard on people with money. Some believe that we are too noisy in worship and wish for more silence. We try to balance these concerns in the movement of our worship service, but there is something very powerful and biblical about such a diverse body gathering around the sacrament of the Lord's Supper, emphasizing in its very presence that it is at the heart of the meaning of the sacrament. When someone asks us if our worship service is a black service or a white service, our answer is that it is neither. That ambiguity is both a blessing and a curse. Our black members will often say that our worship is too "white," while our white members will often say that it is too "black." We seek to help all of us step out into the new reality of Jesus Christ, and that often requires some stretching.

Art

Nowhere is that stretching seen more clearly than in our approach to art. Unlike most of the Protestant and Presbyterian traditions, which have distrusted art as a medium for the holy, at Oakhurst we view art as a portal that provides access to the holy. It is also the most powerful way to help all of us imagine the new reality into which we are called. We have banners in our sanctuary that have been made by our church members. They are there for every season. Only in Lent do we have a barren sanctuary except for a pulpit stole with the cross. Our most controversial move concerning art was in relation to our darkening the skin of Jesus in a stained glass window behind the chancel and pulpit area. The window towers over the front of the sanctuary and is a depiction of the Ascension of Jesus, with angels on each side of him and the male disciples below him.

As we began to gradually grow in the late 1980s, a group of elders on our session began to discuss making changes in our artwork to reflect our diversity. One of the first places on which we focused was the stained glass picture of the Ascension. We actually had two stained glass images of Jesus in the sanctuary, the one of the Ascension in the front and another one of Jesus in the back of the balcony. The portraits of Jesus in both of these were decidedly European. We decided to change the one in the front of the sanctuary since more people would see it. Our session discussed the proposal for change and agreed to it without much dissent. As we began the process, a sense of fear came over us as pastors, for we knew that there would be great resistance.

We decided to use the company who had originally done the windows, and here God's sense of humor came into play. Hoping to avoid a lot of controversy, we had the company come in on Monday to get the panes that needed to be replaced, and they promised us that they would be finished and back in place by Friday. We did this so that the change would be done before anyone would notice. The company kept its promise and got the panes back by Friday, but they looked terrible. We went through Sunday worship with no one mentioning the changes except those on the revision committee. We expressed our dissatisfaction to the company, and they agreed to do the work over. This time, however, they could not get the panes until Thursday, meaning that on the next Sunday, the work would be clear to everyone.

As fate (or providence) would have it, that next Sunday was a special occasion for us as a congregation. One of the white daughters of the church, who had learned to sing as a child growing up in the church, was now an accomplished opera singer, even singing on occasion with the Metropolitan Opera in New York. On this particular Sunday, she was scheduled to sing at the anthem time for us in worship. Many of those who had fled from the church prior to our arrival—and some who had left in response to the changes we initiated—would be coming to worship on this particular Sunday. The singing was, of course, magnificent, but it was done against a background of gaping holes in the stained glass portrait of the Ascension. Now, everyone knew about the change, and everyone would be watching.

The company brought the panes back on Monday, and they were much better. The face, hands, and feet of Jesus were decidedly brown, and included in the disciples now were two dark disciples and a woman. The two white angels were not changed, and we wavered on whether or not to change them also. The matter was settled in one of our session meetings when one of our black elders stated, "I kind of like the idea of white angels bowing to a brown Jesus." The move did cause some controversy, but not nearly as much as we had feared. One long-time white member wrote a letter to the session expressing concern that we had violated the integrity of the art. As we struggled over our response, another of our long-time white elders helped us by telling us that the family who had originally donated the window wanted to take it with them when they left the church because they didn't want black people to violate it.

Our brown-skinned Jesus faces everyone who comes to worship with us, and it has been one of our most powerful evangelical tools. No one who worships with us can escape an encounter with the brown-skinned Jesus. This piece of art causes all of us to feel and to reflect on the power of race in our lives. It is part of the new space that we seek to create in worship. Many of the new members who have joined us since its creation in 1989 have cited the brown-skinned Jesus as the sign to them that our congregation was truly seeking to honor the gift and the power of the diversity that God has created. Almost all of the news media who have done stories on us over the years have been struck by its power. The article in *Time* uses this image as its lead paragraph to captivate the reader:

> At the Oakhurst Presbyterian Church, there's a black Jesus in front, a white Jesus in back and folks of both colors in between. The black Jesus depicted on a stained-glass window in front used to be white, but the pastor of Oakhurst, the Rev. Gibson Stroupe, and his wife Caroline Leach tinted the once pink portrait brown. Both Leach and Stroupe are white, and she admits "we did get some flak" for the racial alteration. There were those who thought Oakhurst was caving in to the dogmatizers of diversity, the whistle blowers of melanin management. Some chose to leave the church and the neighborhood, looking for greener pastures and whiter places in which to live and worship. And then there were those that came, saw and stayed. In a perfect world, religion should be color-blind. Oakhurst isn't in that perfect world. It's in Decatur, Georgia.[9]

Our brown-skinned Jesus is one of our icons, and it is a powerful vehicle for confronting and being confronted by the sacred in our lives. We recently learned, however, why there is hostility in the Protestant tradition about art, especially icons such as our brown-skinned Jesus. Last year we were given a financial donation in memory of one of our first black elders, who had died suddenly. Our session decided to use that donation to repair a lighting system that illuminated our other stained glass portrait of Jesus over the balcony in the back of the sanctuary. This illumination enables the portrait of Jesus to be seen at night throughout the neighborhood, and this portrait is one of a European Jesus, the "white" one described in the *Time* article.

This decision about illumination led to another discussion. Should we project a "white" Jesus in the neighborhood? Should we darken it as we had the other one? Some elders felt that we should darken it, but some liked having two different images of Jesus, one black and one white. We all agreed to look closely at the illuminated image of Jesus over the next month and then to come back to the discussion. At our next session meeting, our brown-skinned icon came under a bit of fire because both white and black elders pointed out that our brown-skinned Jesus was not really a black man—he was rather a man with white features and brown skin. They questioned, then, whether we should do more than darken the skin of the white Jesus—why not make all of his features to be "black," to broaden his nose, thicken his lips, make his hair curly? How could they call our icon into question? It had been such a powerful tool for us to create a broad-based, diverse community of faith! Yet the clarity of their observation could not be ignored or denied, and we decided to continue the discussion about this window to reflect the multicultural community that we are.

We will hear more about our work on the art of our church in chapter 6, but we must note here that it began at the primitive but basic level of Caroline's darkening biblical pictures for Sunday school and has expanded from there. Fortunately for us, denominational materials are beginning to reflect the diversity that is the truth about the biblical witness, but the commitment to diversity still requires a continual search for appropriate materials. As we write this in the Lenten season, we are using African-based drawings of the stations of the cross from a book called *Were You There?*[10]

Christian Education

Caroline coordinates our Christian education program, and here is the place where we have the opportunity to influence children and adults in affirming the gifts of diversity, in offering a view of the new reality that is ours in Jesus Christ, and in proclaiming the stunning news that we are children of God. Caroline, with the help of dedicated church members, has basically built our

Christian education program from the ground up. When we arrived at Oakhurst in 1983, there were no children under ten and very few ages ten to seventeen. We worked hard under Caroline's leadership to recruit children and youth and now have a thriving program. This process is described more fully in chapter 6, but we want to note an observation about our approach made by Foster and Brelsford in their study of us:

> Another important part of the curriculum of this congregation is signified in the phrase "we are all children of God." As their mission statement makes clear, they are "young and old, black and white, employed and unemployed, poor and comfortable, strong and broken." This is the vision and experience of life without dividing walls. "There is lots of love here!" declares one member in an effort to explain what makes this congregation work. "Its like a big family reunion" says another, describing fellowship dinners.
>
> Perhaps many congregations speak of themselves as a family, but this message that "we are all children of God" differs from most family rhetoric. Whereas the notion of family can imply a rigid and unjust hierarchical structure, the notion that we are all children implies a degree of parity among persons and a shared experience of being "childlike." This common experience of being childlike points to the prevalent feeling in this congregation that no one is really in control, even while they take on significant responsibilities. Rather, their life together seems to unfold in ways that cannot be determined in advance. They are not experienced parents guiding others along; they are all eager and ever learning children.
>
> Two aspects, then, of being "children of God" as this congregation understands it are 1) that no one person or group is in charge (serving as the socializing parent), rather, everyone is seen as relatively naïve and inexperienced; and 2) the future is seen as unfolding out of the collective interacting of the members of the family, rather than being decided by "parents" or leaders. [11]

Another of our anchors in Christian education is learning the Bible, the sacred text of the church. Like many others, we lament the biblical illiteracy in our time, and we seek to make the sacred text the center of our curriculum. We do this not as biblical literalists, for such a vantage point seems full of holes to us. In the first place, there is not even an accepted "Bible" in Christendom—there is a Protestant Bible, a Roman Catholic Bible, an Orthodox Bible, and other versions. Which of these is the authentic "Bible" depends, of course, on one's own heritage. And second, the purpose of the Bible seems to us not to be a rule book like a code of law but rather a map of the spiritual journey with God. Our approach is that the Bible is a sacred text because it is a primary place for meeting God. In the Bible we meet God, and we meet ourselves. The Bible is a collection of the history of a people and of individuals who have hungered for God, who have often fed their hunger with junk food, but who have continued to be called and redeemed by God. The diversity of our congregation reflects the various approaches and points of view—people with Ph.D. degrees in biblical studies, people who can hardly read, people who know very little about the Bible.

We have weekly Bible study in which we seek to find God's truth for us in the sacred texts and in our reflections on and discussions of those texts. Our regular participants bring a wide range of backgrounds. One was a medical student at Emory who was raised in the Roman Catholic tradition and knew very little about the Bible. We still remember her shock when we read in the third chapter of Mark that Jesus' family had come to visit him. "You mean Jesus had sisters?" She asked. "I thought he was the only one." Other participants are getting doctoral degrees in biblical studies. We have men and women, black and white—a great variety of folk who have a great variety of reactions to the biblical stories.

In the Bible study, we seek not to find the one true answer of the meaning of the text. We search for a core meaning, but we also recognize the value of hearing and honoring the impact that biblical stories have on particular people. Our purpose is not to get people to agree on the meaning of a particular text. It is rather to seek to open up the text so that each of us and all of us can meet God there. Rather than leading to a relativism of biblical interpretation, we have found that this approach produces powerful insights about who God is and how God speaks and acts in our lives.

A couple of years ago, one of our student interns in ministry was leading a session in our Bible study as we worked our way through the book of Judges. Most of our participants that night were women. She was leading us through the nineteenth chapter of Judges, a gruesome chapter. The story concerns a Levite who is taking his concubine back home and is staying the night in Gibeah of the tribe of Benjamin. Hearing that there is a stranger in the house, the men of the town decide to humiliate him by raping him. The owner of the house will not let his guest outside but offers his virgin daughter and the guest's concubine instead. Finally, the concubine is pushed out the door and is raped repeatedly through the night. As dawn breaks, she crawls back to the threshold of the door and dies. The Levite then cuts her body into twelve pieces and sends it to the tribes of Israel, seeking to provoke revenge upon the men of Gibeah.

Nibs was a part of this Bible study, and though he was not leading it, he had anticipated that the discussion would center on homosexuality and whether or not this passage was meant to condemn it. He had prepared for this direction and had reviewed some of the commentaries concerning homosexuality. He could not have been more wrong. After the passage was read aloud, there was a long silence. The rape of the woman and the desecration of her body put us in a zone where the sacrilege seemed profound. Finally, one woman spoke up: "I can feel the knife cutting up my body." Then another woman: "I can't believe that they just threw her out there to be raped." And another: "And the man offered his daughter, too. Wasn't she of any value?" Tears were coming down many cheeks, and Nibs perceived that we were on holy ground. This story, as gruesome as it was, had opened a window into the hearts and minds of the women gathered for Bible study, a window for them to acknowledge the pain and anger and frustration of being treated as an object to be used and abused. Our student intern, though less "trained" than Nibs, did a skillful job of leading us through a difficult but holy experience. She did so well because she had received "on the job training" as a woman in a society that sought to demean her humanity. And, though he kept it to himself, Nibs was surprised at the depth of feeling among these women and was astonished at how much he had missed a core meaning of this passage: when women are seen as less than human, the story in Judges 19 is the result. It was a powerful lesson to Nibs about how much his own context determined the way he approached Scripture and about how much he needed to hear the other perspectives. The truth of this passage was not so much one of correct interpretation as it was the invitation to listen to the stories of others and of where the text spoke to them in their contexts.

On another occasion, the Bible study group was beginning a study of the book of Daniel. In the first chapter, we read a quick summary of the Babylonian conquest of Jerusalem and the subsequent exile. Daniel is one of four young Israelites selected by the king's staff to be groomed for duty in the king's court, no doubt as translators and agents of the king among the Israelites. They are given royal food to eat, but Daniel and the others refused to eat the king's food because they did not want to defile themselves. During our discussion of their refusal to eat the Babylonian food, we wondered about the Jewish food laws that play such a prominent role throughout the Biblical witness. It was noted that the food laws enabled Jews to retain their identity, no matter where their Diaspora took them.

One of the young men in our group, who is a doctoral candidate in Christian ethics at Emory University, spoke about the power of this passage for him. He understood Daniel's resistance because he felt the same pressure at Emory. The offering of food to Daniel and the others was just a small step, but it had huge implications. The movement in the academy was to encourage this doctoral student to accept its view on a gradual basis rather than in a gargantuan conversation—baby steps that one doesn't remember, small crossings that grow larger after one steps over them. The young man appreciated Daniel's resistance to taking this first step, and we were impressed by this insight into how the powers and principalities work in our lives. It is rare that the powers roll over us like a tank in battle. Rather, it is more like a piece of candy offered to us casually, seemingly without any strings attached, until the daily dose of candy becomes a necessity of life, and we cannot even remember how it got to be that way. It was a profound insight into this biblical passage and opened up meanings and voices that we had not connected with the passage.

As we moved into the New Testament, we began a reading of Luke's Gospel. The first ten verses of Luke 7 have an encounter between Jesus and a centurion in Capernaum. The story is about the authority of Jesus and the faith that the centurion has in that authority. The centurion has a slave whom he values highly but who is dying. He sends word to Jesus through Jewish elders, asking Jesus to come and heal his slave. As Jesus approaches his house, the centurion sends word to Jesus not to come for he is not worthy to have Jesus enter his house. He requests that Jesus command his slave to be healed from where Jesus stands, knowing that the authority of Jesus is so great that it would be done. Jesus is amazed at the centurion's faith and contrasts it with the faith of the people of Israel—and the slave is healed.

As we began our discussion on this passage, we intended to take it toward such issues as faith healing, the power of faith, and whether this really happened in quite this way or whether it had been considerably embellished in the telling of it through the tradition. We also thought the contrast between the centurion's faith and that of Israel might be worth exploring. The African American folk in our study, however, raised another issue: Why didn't Jesus order the centurion to free his slave? Did this passage mean that Jesus gave implicit if not explicit blessings to the institution of slavery? Was the mission of Jesus to change society or was it just a mission to individuals? Was his mission to heal individuals such as this slave without healing the society that created the sickness called slavery?

Those of us who were white had accepted slavery as part of the social landscape of this passage, part of the background to the real meaning and power of the story. Those who were black had a different approach—the real meaning and power of this story centered on slavery and Jesus' opinion of slavery. We had a lively discussion as we noted the differences between Roman slavery and American slavery and as we noted the ambivalence of the biblical witness on the issue of slavery. In Deut. 23:15 we find that runaway slaves are not to be returned to their masters, while in Philemon, Paul is returning a runaway slave but is urging Philemon to grant him freedom. Paul also emphasizes obedience to masters by slaves (Colossians 3 and Ephesians 6), but in Galatians 5 urges all Christians not to allow themselves to become slaves.

It was yet another example of the power of the sacred texts to grab us where we are and of the power of our social context, which is a huge determining factor in how we perceive and receive the biblical texts. It was also a reminder of how central the Bible has been in the debate about slavery in the United States. Nibs has a book on his shelf given to him by his great-great aunt, who helped to raise him. It was published in 1857 and is entitled *The Great Question Answered, or Is Slavery a Sin in Itself?* It was written by James A. Sloan and claims to produce the biblical and theological justification for slavery.

One final example should accentuate the flavor and power of our Bible study. In that same seventh chapter of Luke, we read the story of a woman of the city who invaded the Pharisee's house to anoint Jesus and to wash and wipe his feet with her kisses and her hair. This story is found in some form in all four Gospel accounts and is often identified with Mary Magdalene, though none of the Gospels provide that identification. While the men in our Bible study mentioned the erotic images of this woman rubbing Jesus and wiping him with her hair, the women reminded us that we had missed the point; the passage was not about sex at all. They noted that the Pharisee thinks that it is sexual and is offended. The women were moved, however, by the affirmation of the humanity of the woman by Jesus. "Do you see this woman?" Jesus asks the Pharisee in order to point out to him that he didn't "see" the woman. The Pharisee saw her as a sex object, a piece of property that belonged to men, and offensive property at that.

The women in our group acknowledged the physical power of this story with the touching of bodies, but they also reminded us men that because for men sexuality is usually limited to the genitals, men could not perceive how grateful this woman was to Jesus for acknowledging her as a sister, as a person with possibilities. They emphasized that the woman was indeed pouring her whole being into Jesus not in order to seduce him but as a way of saying "thank you." It was sexual in that they were touching but it was not an invitation to have sexual intercourse. It was rather a pouring out of passion to thank Jesus for his invitation to her to come into the circle of humanity.

These examples from our Bible study give a glimpse of the high respect we have for the biblical texts and for the Reformed principle that the meaning and truth of the texts are to be found in community. The individual must have access to the texts in order that we may know the sacred stories, but it is only in dialogue with others that our own individual perspectives and limitations are acknowledged and broadened. It is only in dialogue that the meaning and the truth of the texts can be discerned. One of the great gifts for us in our approach to the biblical texts is the diversity of our congregation, a diversity that helps open up differing perspectives on the power of the biblical stories. In this way it is reinforced over and over again that our own particular story is important but that it is only part of the story. It is only in encountering the important stories of others that we can really begin to glimpse the depth and immensity and mystery of the Story.

Chapter Five

Out into the World: The Importance of Public Ministry

The ongoing witness of the congregation's very existence as a racially diverse community of faith in an environment of racial tensions both attracts and repels people in the neighborhood and city. The impetus for such action comes from the congregation's awareness not only of the bad news of racism, for alone that provides no hope but also of the good news of Jesus Christ.

—C. Foster & T. Brelsford[1]

We believe that our life together calls us to examine both our inner space and our outer space. We are called to go below the surface of our lives to find where the powers and principalities have so captured parts of ourselves that it becomes difficult to even imagine the possibility of the reality of the God movement. A prime place for testing out that captivity and the new reality is in our outer space, in our relation to others. Jesus took this approach in his ministry. He summarized the entire corpus of the law and the prophets into two commandments: "You shall love the Lord your God with all your heart and with all your soul and with all your mind" and "You shall love your neighbor as yourself" (Matt. 22:34–40). In this summary, Jesus emphasizes that God is the center of our lives, and our calling is to acknowledge that God is the center of our lives. Jesus was well aware, however, that our usual response is to try to juggle God and the lesser gods at the center of our lives. In order to counter this tendency, Jesus adds a second commandment that lifts up the neighbor as the litmus test for whether or not we have centered ourselves on God. In trying to assure ourselves that we have put God at the center of our lives, we often seek to reshape God in our image rather than reshaping ourselves in God's image.

Jesus offers us assistance in confronting and extricating ourselves from this deadly trap. How do we know if we are loving God "with all our heart and soul and mind?" We can judge that by how we relate to our neighbor. Who is our neighbor? It is the same question that a lawyer asked Jesus in Luke 10, centered on this same issue of the summary of the law and the prophets. Jesus answers the question by telling the story of the Good Samaritan, indicating that our neighbors are not just the folks we know and trust but also those that we have been told are our enemy. Jesus suggests that the only way we can measure how we are relating to God is in how we are relating to our neighbor and not just the neighbor that we like.

At the heart of our life together at Oakhurst is an attempt to weave together a community ministry that incorporates this approach, one that weaves together both justice and mercy. Both of these components are necessary for sustaining viable community ministry. Our community ministry is also a strong evangelism proclamation for us. We attract and keep many folk who hear about and who experience our community ministry. One of our veteran members put it this way: "I used to attend a Baptist church but I wanted to attend a church that was more active in the community. . . . [T]his church [Oakhurst] had an outreach program and that was how I got started here. . . . I was really impressed with their involvement in the community. . . . [T]he Baptist church seemed like it was in chaos . . . like it was all about money . . . every Sunday people would come in a new outfit, stay in church until 3:00, and then the same thing the next Sunday with nothing done in between. . . . [T]his church really does make a difference in the community."[2]

Our community ministry seeks to incorporate both justice and charity. Both are necessary and must supplement each other if either is to be viable. At the root of the Christian life are works of charity: "I was hungry, and you fed me; I was thirsty, and you gave me drink." We have many of these works of charity in our midst: our clothes closet is the only metro-wide one that accepts walk-in participants. We share in our presbytery's hunger program, for which our giving is the highest per capita in the presbytery. We also have a tutoring program that assists elementary and middle-school children, a weekly AA meeting, and a senior citizens program that meets for exercise, fellowship, and community discussion. Over fifty community groups used our facilities last year. We thus have a thriving community ministry that seeks to meet both physical and spiritual needs of the community, both for the local neighborhood and city-wide.

Oakhurst has always had a history of being involved in its community. As we saw in chapter 1, Jack and Joy Morris helped to revive this tradition after it had subsided in the white flight. That revival lasted for awhile, but it too began to dwindle a few years after their departure. By the time we arrived as pastors, the community ministry had shrunk considerably—only the Metro

Girls Club remained as a legacy of the Morris's work. Other than that, every door to every room seemed like it was locked. Because of the work of the Morris pastorate, though, we knew that the legacy and the spark of serving the community remained viable. We began to seek ways to build on that base and that legacy. Our strategy was to open up the building and to proclaim to the community that we were there to serve them in the name of Christ. We were not looking so much for new members as were looking to give evidence that there was life in the building. Caroline led and coordinated our efforts in community ministry.

We became a center for distribution of commodity food from the federal government to people in need. Every two months, we would have eight hundred to a thousand people come into the church during the week of food distribution, and we had to have community volunteers to help distribute the food. There was some initial grumbling about the kinds of people who came in for the program, but the sessional leadership stood behind it. This program stayed with us for two years until an evaluation claimed that we gave away too much food! In the meantime, an educator on the staff of a nearby Presbyterian church came to us seeking space for a Head Start program on whose board he served. It would bring in forty to sixty children every day. We were enthusiastic, and although there was some resistance on the session because of security and building concerns, the elders voted to allow the program. It was a great boon to us because the building came alive every day, and it provided great space for a government program that has been highly acclaimed. This program, which began at our church in 1985 and lasted until 1993, provided a base for many other types of community ministry.

We also moved on other fronts. A community group came to us in 1985 looking for space for a shelter for women with children because there was very little space available for them in the entire metro area. Again the session had a difficult struggle over safety issues, but fortunately for us, we had also just begun a student intern program with nearby Columbia Theological Seminary. Our first student, Bob Reno, was willing to oversee the program, and our elders agreed to house it on a temporary basis in our fellowship hall. Thus, the transformation had begun from a building with every door locked to a building with the doors flung wide open—to preschool children and folk needing food by day and to women and children needing shelter by night. Our space for the shelter was woefully inadequate, but it did help its organizers see the possibilities. The local fire department tolerated it for awhile because of the great need, but since we were violating almost every fire code, they eventually gave us a deadline for closing the shelter. By that time, the shelter had outgrown our space and had found new space, and several other church-sponsored shelters have now sprung up from our initial efforts.

Using our Head Start base of children and families, we also began an adult literacy program. We partnered with our local county school board: they provided the teachers several days a week, and we provided the space and recruited the students. We had many kinds of folk come to this program—older adults who wanted to learn to read the Bible, refugees wanting to learn to read English, and high school dropouts wanting to prepare for their GED test. We saw a great need for child care for this program, so we hired certified preschool teachers to work with the children while their parents received literacy training. We also partnered with a counselor at Decatur High School to work with at-risk youth, and we started the Decatur Youth Business Organization to help teach employment skills to these youth and to help them work on their academic skills. Because the school system was skeptical about this program, it was housed initially at our church until it grew too large for us to handle. By this time, it had won several community service awards, and the local school system was ready to take it over.

In all of these programs, we demonstrated to our membership that it was possible to have poor and black people come into the building without destroying it or causing great problems. There were definitely tensions and conflicts and minor disturbances but none of great consequence. We did experience an increase in the number of break-ins, so much so that we rarely ever left anything of value in the building. We debated over whether to get a burglar alarm system, but we as pastors were strongly opposed because we felt that it sent the wrong message about our hospitality. In the fall of 1988, however, we had break-ins every two weeks or so, with the final straw being the theft of over three hundred Christmas presents earmarked for the Head Start children. We yielded in our opposition to the alarm and had one installed, and it greatly reduced the number of break-ins.

While our membership began to see the benefits of a life-filled building during the week, the community began to see us as its community center—the place where their lives and their experiences were valued, a place of advocacy for community issues. The word about our community ministry began to spread all over the city. One crucial element was funding, which we needed for staffing and for program and building expenses. For many years, Atlanta Presbytery and its successor Greater Atlanta Presbytery have underwritten partnership funding for our ministries. It is no exaggeration to say that without the spiritual and financial support of the Presbytery Oakhurst would not have survived. When we came to Oakhurst as pastors, the executive presbyter said that he would support funding for Oakhurst for two more years. He was not even enthusiastic about that, but because of our reputation as urban ministers, he was willing to try it a bit longer. That support has obviously continued, for which we give thanks. We are also thankful for the shift from a "welfare" mentality in the presbytery, which saw funding to churches like Oakhurst as helping the underprivileged who could not help themselves, to a "partnership" mentality, which sees church funding as mission work, carrying out the mission of the presbytery.

We are grateful for presbytery's support, but we also had to go out and find other funding. We received a portion of our denomination's Presbyterian Women Thank Offering in 1989 for our community ministry, and out of that we created a non-profit organization that can receive secular funding. We have been fortunate to receive continued funding from local Presbyterian churches such as Trinity, Clairmont, and Decatur and broader religious organizations such as Church Women United. We also received funding from local arts councils and from the state and local governments related to health issues and teens and have had numerous fund-raisers, such as yard sales, food sales, and gospel concerts.

Our mission to take the gospel out into the world has not only touched the lives of the neighborhood but our own membership as well. A significant percentage of our members are poor and black and thus are often crunched by the institutions of our society. We have been in the middle of their journeys, seeking to help them survive that crunch. We have sometimes, however, made mistakes by bringing a "white" point of view to certain situations—sometimes blaming the black man in the family for the problem, sometimes expecting the families to have middle-class goals. Yet we are always advocates for people caught up in the systems of our society—the educational system, the judicial system, the healthcare system, and many others. Even in the midst of our confusion and mixed motives, we have found that an advocate is better than none at all.

On one occasion one of our African American members called on us to help her with her son, who had been arrested for selling drugs. Since we knew that he would be merely fodder for the system, we went to work as a church with our contacts and found a place for him in a drug diversion program. We ascertained that he was not using drugs but was rather selling them. He stayed for ninety days in the diversion program and was released on probation. He has been clean ever since, a period of over seven years. On another occasion, one of our African American adults called Nibs seeking assistance with a difficulty on the grand jury system. She had agreed to serve on the grand jury panel but had become disgusted with the racism that she encountered there—with black women being called "whores" and with the assumption that most of the black men who had been arrested were actually guilty. She told the district attorney that she wanted to get off the grand jury because of the racism, but he told her that she would be held in contempt of court if she did not complete her term. She called Nibs, and together they negotiated her departure.

Several of our families have been affected by the drug use of their parents, and we as a church have stepped in to assist in these situations. On one occasion, the mother of two girls went out on the street on drugs, and eventually one of our members took the girls into their home. On another occasion, a young girl's mother was selling drugs out of her home and sometimes selling her own body. We helped to get the girl out of that situation and into another home, and she just recently graduated from nursing school.

At the heart of our life are these works of charity and mercy. They are essential works of discipline for the Christian journey. They not only provide assistance for those in need and thus help complete God's providential work; they also deepen those assisting, who receive gifts by having their hearts and minds opened to the places where the principalities and powers have captured them and society's institutions. They also begin to see the intersections of the works of mercy and the call to justice. As the Brazilian theologian Dom Helder Camara once put it, "When I gave food to the poor, they called me a saint. When I asked why the poor had no food, they called me a communist."[3] Camara challenges us all to think outside the box, to ask why we have all accepted the capitalist assumption about life that ties public policy to ability to pay. Our life together at Oakhurst causes us to challenge many of the assumptions that we bring to the lives of others.

In this intersection of charity and justice, we are led into dialogue, and at times confrontation, with the institutions of society. Because of our involvement with our own members at Oakhurst, we are led to ask fundamental questions of ourselves and of society: Why is it our public policy in the United States to have hungry people? Why is it our public policy to lock up black males? Why is it our public policy to have homeless people? Why is it our public policy to deny decent health care to so many in our society? We recognize that works of charity and mercy are absolutely essential to our life together, but we also recognize that works of justice are essential. In this regard, we are often out in the middle of the struggles in the world.

We joined the Open Door Community in picketing another Presbyterian church in Atlanta that was ousting homeless people sleeping on its doorsteps, and we eventually led the civil disobedience that took their "No Trespassing" signs down. Our leadership is central in our presbytery's Committee to Combat Racism, and we helped coordinate the presbytery's passage of a strong antiracism mission statement. We have been at the forefront of a campaign to develop affordable housing in our community and to insist that the city of Decatur find ways to assist elderly residents of Oakhurst in paying their property taxes in a rapidly escalating real estate market. Some of our members have received death threats at work because of their stands against racism at their places of employment. We again assisted the Open Door in its takeover of an old, abandoned hotel in downtown Atlanta, a move that resulted in the promise of three thousand beds for homeless people. That very hotel is now the site of affordable housing. We have a public policy advocate in our congregation, and she keeps us apprised of the issues before the state legislature. Recently, she requested that we voice our concern over a bill to slightly diminish the power of predatory lending, and we flooded offices with phone calls and faxes. As a result of our efforts and those of many other groups, in 2002, the Georgia legislature passed the strongest state law against predatory lending in the country. We are often asked by community groups to assist them in their work for justice.

Doing works of mercy and charity is difficult enough, but moving into works of justice is often frightening because the issues are so complex. Many groups and churches do works of mercy and call that "justice," but we persist in connecting the two and see both as necessary in order to take the gospel out into the world. The works of justice often require us to move into murky areas where the lines between good and evil sometimes become blurred, into difficult areas where we often face a choice between lesser evils and lesser goods. It is in these areas that church people have a difficult time working, and rightly so, for we often find ourselves aligning with those about whom we are not so sure. Yet sometimes these alliances must be made, and in so doing, we often find the humanity of those we thought were completely alien.

We lead many workshops on the continuing power of racism and on how to combat that power. It is in such workshops that these issues become focused most clearly. In Presbyterian groups, we often have to confront the difficult truth that it is our elders and members who implement and maintain the power of racism in such areas as education, banking, health care, and the criminal justice system. It is important to be advocates for our individuals caught up in these systems so that racism will have less power in them. In our workshops, team members often ask difficult questions of ourselves and of the other participants, questions designed to raise the issue of race: Where do we live? Where do we worship? What schools do our children attend? Why did we choose those schools? Where do we play? It only takes a few of these questions for the hostility and defensiveness to rise in the room, but it is an exercise that seeks to focus the problem and bring us all to awareness of how much we have been captured by the power of race.

Our works of mercy and justice often take us into difficult areas as we seek to proclaim the good news that God has broken down the dividing walls of hostility. We have come to learn that "breaking down the dividing walls" is not an easy or gentle metaphor—it rather describes the shattering of a boundary marker. Despite Robert Frost's assertion that "good fences make good neighbors," we also acknowledge the truth of the line in that same poem: "Something there is that doesn't love a wall."[4] When working for justice, we expect conflict and harsh reactions to the call for the shattering of the dividing walls. In this process, we seek to demonstrate not how righteous we are and how unrighteous the others are but rather how much the principalities and powers have captured all of our hearts and our minds and our imaginations—as well as the institutions that grow out of this captivity and reinforce it.

In this process our goal is to proclaim the good news of the mediating presence of the God we know in Jesus Christ. We proclaim that God is calling us to give up our dependence on race, on male domination, on materialism, and on many other idols—giving these up not so that we'll be good and pure but so that we can experience the glorious freedom of the children of God. In this sense, what often sounds initially like bad news to us and to others is in actuality good news that will bring us life and hope. This good news is at the heart of our community ministry, of our attempts to take the gospel out into the world.

Our impetus for this movement was the dramatic change in our community that resulted from white people fleeing in massive numbers from the black people who were moving in. The idols revealed in that mass exodus have continued to be a central focus for us in our ministry. Now we face another dramatic change in our neighborhood, a change coming not as quickly as the previous one but coming nevertheless. Six or seven years ago we noticed an inrease in the number of white people moving in. As we are writing this, we do not yet have the results of the 2000 census, but we are guessing that the numbers will show a dramatic rise in the number of white people in the neighborhood.

Why would white people move into a neighborhood that was vastly black? It seemed to go against the power of racism that we have cited repeatedly. Yet as we reflected on this movement, the reasons became clearer. Our neighborhood was part of the white movement back into the city that is happening all over the nation. Our particular transition has been fueled by low housing prices, depressed because it has been a black neighborhood. The housing stock itself is relatively good, making a combination for great profit. And huge profits there have been. For years little capital was available for home improvement, but now that white people are moving in, there has been a huge surge in the flow of capital. The huge profits to be made here because of the depressed market have brought many speculators into the neighborhood.

Another reason for the increase in white residents is easy access to the nearby rapid transit system. There is a MARTA station two blocks north of our church, and many white workers, tired of commuting for hours each day in their cars, have moved into the city to have easy access to mass transmit. It reflects a growing distaste for commuting by automobile: until early 2001, people in the Atlanta area drove further in daily commutes than people in any other metropolitan area in the country. People are also attracted to the city of Decatur, a bedroom community for Atlanta that calls itself "Mayberry" even though forty per cent of its residents are black. (We grew up watching the "Andy Griffith Show" on television, whose fictional town was Mayberry, and do not recall ever seeing a black person on the show.) Nevertheless, Decatur has become an "in" place to live, and our neighborhood is the cheapest one in the city. The crime rate is also low all over Decatur.

This last reason reflects an influence of a mammoth redevelopment project about one mile south of our church in which a wealthy white developer persuaded the Atlanta Housing Authority to let him acquire a large public housing project in the name of "tearing down the neighborhood to save it." This move was done to help restore the glory of a former white country club and a golf course designed originally by Bobby Jones. In the name of progress and decency, at least seven hundred families lost their homes so that white capital could feel safe to speculate in our neighborhood. It was all done, of course, in the name of helping and revitalizing the neighborhood, all the while depicting the residents of the housing project as people who could not handle life at best and criminals at worst. With the removal of this housing project and its 99 percent black population, white people felt safer putting their bodies and their money in the neighborhood. On a smaller scale, about a mile north of the church, eighty units of low-income housing were taken last fall—this time, however, there was at least honesty about the motivation—"Rich people want the land."[5] There was no attempt to portray the poor people who lived there as bad as was done in the development to the south—just an emphasis on economic and market forces. What can you do about those, anyway?

Our community seeks to proclaim that economic and market forces are not ultimate; rather, God's power and grace are ultimate. In the midst of this proclamation, we are not certain what this transition will mean for us over the long haul. As one of our black members put it, "Oakhurst may be the first multicultural church to turn white." It is true that most multicultural churches eventually lose most of their white membership, but the demographics of our neighborhood seem to indicate otherwise. We receive many new white visitors in worship, and some of the new white residents have become members. Yet there are downsides for us also. Many black residents of the neighborhood are leaving, some because of the huge profits they can make on their houses, some because they are driven out by rapidly escalating rents or property taxes that they cannot afford to pay. This has not hurt us as much as it might have because our membership is not based just in our neighborhood. Still, though the majority of our membership at the beginning of 2001 was black by a slender margin, by the end of 2002 we anticipate a majority who are white.

We are also seeking to discern ways to minister to our new white neighbors. Many of them are children of the Reagan revolution that put materialism and money and meritocracy at the center of life. Many of them believe that racism was banished by the civil rights movement and that it does not reside in their hearts as it did in the hearts of their forebears. We did start a neighborhood association that seeks to foster dialogue between white and black neighbors, but many of the black folk have dropped out of it because they find the disavowal of racism by the white folk difficult to swallow. In an ironic twist for us, we at Oakhurst find ourselves just as perplexed about ministry to the new white residents as our forebears were perplexed about ministry to the new black residents who came to the neighborhood thirty years ago.

We are a church that has known and that continues to know the movement of the city. Just as we counted on God to lead us in the earlier transition, so shall we do it in this current transition. We are ever mindful that God often surprises us and that God has a sense of humor. Early in the 1990s the vast majority of members that we were receiving were black, and at some point in that process we thought, "Here we go—we are following the usual pattern for multicultural churches, going from white to multicultural to ethnic." Yet here we are now, concerned about the exact opposite! Whatever God has in store for us here at Oakhurst, we will seek to trust in God and to proclaim the gospel. We will continue to take our proclamation out into the world.

Chapter Six

Who Are These People?:
Stories of Our Members

You come and you could be sitting next to a doctor, a lawyer, a home-
less person or a professor. But they're just "Bob." You'd never know
it. None of that matters, we're all just here.

—Loretta Jefferson

*T*he epigraph is a quote from one of our African American young adults who
has been part of Oakhurst since her early teens.[1] In the Introduction, we mentioned the second chapter of Acts, in which the followers of Jesus begin to
demonstrate the mighty power of God on Pentecost. The reaction of the crowds
gathered in Jerusalem for the festival is one of amazement—Who are these
people? The same question is asked about us at Oakhurst—Who are these people? The answer is, "We're all just here." We're all here because we have this
hunger in our hearts, this hunger to hear that we are children of God, this hunger
to know that we are loved, this hunger to know and to be known. We're all here
because we have begun to experience a sense of being a child of God at
Oakhurst, a sense of being defined by God and not by the powers of the world.

We are blessed with all kinds of people at Oakhurst, all kinds of categories,
a great garden of many different types of people. We have people who have
finally found a place where they can put their fire into the faith, where they
can express their passion for God. We have people who have been severely
wounded and are looking for healing, are hoping to find restoration and
wholeness and reconciliation with God. We have people from "mixed race"
families who are looking for a place where they can all feel welcomed. We
have people who have been turned off by the growing emphasis in the black
church on materialism as the answer to questions of justice. We have people
who have been alienated from the white church's emphasis on spirituality
at the expense of justice. We have people in mental and physical distress—
hearing voices, bipolar, brain-injured—looking to hear that God still claims

them and that God has work for them to do. We have gay and lesbian couples looking for a place that affirms God's "Yes" to them. Twenty-one of our members have Ph.D. degrees or are working towards them. We have nine ministers who are retired or are working in other places who are part of our community of faith. We have people who are illiterate and people who barely graduated from high school.

We seek to make it clear at Oakhurst that all of us come to God in distress, that none of us has our act together, that we are all wounded. We do this not to flog ourselves but rather to seek to be realistic about ourselves and our lives. We seek to find a measure of healing in our woundedness, and, in so doing, to begin to become "wounded healers."[2] We seek to share—some of us reluctantly—the truth that our hearts long for God, and we seek to build rituals and a community in which both our weaknesses and our strengths can be acknowledged and affirmed.

In this chapter you will gain glimpses of our membership, most speaking in their own words from articles and interviews and letters. All of us want to bring our fire to Oakhurst, to find a place where we can finally say, "Yes" to God without feeling ashamed or repressed. All of us also bring our fears to Oakhurst, how much we are afraid of saying, "Yes" to God, how much we are afraid of encountering those who are markedly different from us, how much we are afraid of being exposed in our captivity to the powers. At Oakhurst we find a place where we can express both our fire and our fear.

In this chapter we will share brief portraits and the words of some of the members of Oakhurst. Space limitations mean that we can share only a few; but in truth the Oakhurst story is the story of people coming here, wanting to have their story met by The Story. It is the story of people moving out of their comfort zones to encounter the other and finding both discomfort and great gifts. As one of our members put it; "You can find just about any story at Oakhurst. You never know what kind of person lies behind the exterior covering." That has been our discovery and our strength—to find a place where we can be ourselves and encounter the living God. Here's how one of our members put it:

Since Chelsea was young, I have been searching for a church home in Atlanta. Every few weeks I would visit another congregation that I thought might fit. Many were nice, but not what I was looking for. I wanted a church that was racially mixed, where my family's racial diversity would not be tolerated or ignored, but embraced. I hoped to find a place that was not so liberal they were afraid to talk about God, but not so conservative that I would have to struggle to find God in their message.

Although it didn't seem like a lot to ask for, after several years of on and

off effort, I was about ready to give up hope. However, a series of coinci-
dences brought me to Oakhurst. On the first Sunday that Chelsea, Adrian
and I walked in the door, we were greeted with the beautiful image of a
brown Jesus staring down on us. Chelsea and I looked at that Jesus, then
looked at each other and smiled, for we knew we had found our church. The
greatest irony is that my lengthy search throughout the city landed me at a
church less than a mile from my home.[3]

We have families of "mixed races," a category of the world that tells them
that they should not be together, as the label "mixed" implies. In our space
they can find safe haven, space where they are free to be themselves. In our
space they can hear that their primary definition is child of God. There have
been tensions around this issue in our history as a church. Our first multiracial couples usually were a black man and a white woman. Soon after the first
multiracial couple joined as members, one of the black women asked Nibs,
"Am I going to have to see this every Sunday? Couldn't he have found a sister to marry?" Those tensions have lessened as the mixtures change, and our
mixtures now include white men and black women, Asian and black, Hispanic
and black. The tensions have also lessened as people have gotten to know one
another. Being in one another's presence has helped break down the categories of the world. We affirm the variety and the diversity that God has created, and when those varieties gather in families, we see that as a strength and
a hope rather than a problem.

Surely God must smile whenever people gather at Oakhurst! Just as we
rejoice at the birth of a child, God must rejoice in the promise of your testimony. While visiting your worship this past April 20th, I witnessed a
remarkable community of love and fellowship. Your congregation is a wonderful confirmation of the potential of the fruits of the Spirit in action. What
is happening at Oakhurst is the embodiment of what God must have
intended the Church to be—a community of believers faithfully responding
to Christ's teachings. Since our visit I have often imagined what would happen if every community had just one Church like Oakhurst. How quickly
we would begin to overcome our prejudice born of fear and ignorance. How
we might begin to respect our differences and celebrate the fact that all of
God's children are members of the same family. How much easier it would
be for each of us to love our brothers and sisters in our communities and all
over this planet.[4]

This letter is from a man in South Carolina, the father of one of our regular participants in worship. It captures the impact that Oakhurst can have on
people, whether they visit us one time, as this letter writer did, or whether they

are members of Oakhurst. Another visitor, who included us in his sermon to his congregation in Ontario after worshiping with us during his two-week study leave, reflected on the words of an Oakhurst member: "Now, let me assure you, I have heard and read a lot of words these past two weeks. But ten words of hers stand out above all the rest: "Worship at Oakhurst is the sanest part of my week.""[5]

"Worship at Oakhurst is the sanest part of my week." We do try to provide space for people to come and bring all of themselves—their hopes, their dreams, their fears, their fire, their passion, their sorrows, their disappointments, their longings—and have themselves and their deepest parts met by the grace of God. In a crazy world that seeks to build a hierarchy of domination—of men over women, of rich over poor, of white over everyone else—in this kind of world, life at Oakhurst often is a place to find our center, to find our vision, to find our sanity.

One of our members, an African American man who is a seminary student, writes of his struggles with the craziness of the world:

> Thank you very much for all you folks have done for me. Having Oakhurst is part of what helps me survive this madness. . . . Nibs, the "whiteboys" at the Center Psychological Blah Blah Blah, said my exam showed me to be a little paranoid! I laughed my rear end off!
>
> They asked a brother . . . , "Do you ever feel like people are watching you? And do you feel like people are trying to influence or control your thoughts?" They asked a black man, "If you felt like people said insulting things about you? or If some folks were working against you?" Nibs I am serious; everyone of those questions was on that psychological evaluation! And my YESES sent up red flags! What brother would not test paranoid in America on a white exam designed 30 years ago? Lawd have mercy![6]

This man was a businessman in our community whom we met in helping to set up a community development corporation. He had gone to Morehouse College for a year but ran out of money and went into business for himself. He was a magnet for African American teens and began to help us see their needs and to structure our community ministry programs in response to those needs. He also alerted us, in the early stages of gentrification, of the issues that were emerging as young whites moved into the neighborhood and as the city suddenly "discovered" the Oakhurst community because of the growing presence of young white people. As we worked together on many fronts, he became more and more attracted to our church and eventually joined. His mother is a pastor, and he had grown up in the Pentecostal tradition, but he found himself joining with us because of our weaving of spirituality and justice. During this part of the journey, he began to discover a calling to ministry that he had long suppressed, and he began to affirm the possibility of going into the ministry, even as a Presbyterian, or at least as a "Bapti-Pentaterian" as he put it. To go in this direction meant to finish college and then to go to seminary; it meant to give up his business and go to the edge economically. His work in the community and his journey at Oakhurst confirmed his calling, however, and he returned to Morehouse and graduated, and is now in seminary, trying to weave his black consciousness with being a Presbyterian in a white denomination. Oakhurst serves as both an anchor and a vision for him in that journey.

We also serve as an entry point back into the church for many people who long for the church but have been alienated from it. Some have left the church because they are angry at God. Others have left because they have experienced it as a place where passion is repressed rather than expressed. Some have been repulsed by the church's racism, sexism, and homophobia, and some have left because of their own inner struggles. Some see the church as an exclusive club that seeks to condemn those who are excluded, and some have experienced it as a place that seeks to capture God rather than expressing thanks to God. Others see it as an institution that often blesses the injustice in the world. And some have left the church because they have been captured by the powers of the world.

We have many seekers among our members at Oakhurst, and we welcome all to bring their questions and their struggles. We do this because we affirm that God wants our passion, not our perfection. Here are the reflections of one of those seekers who is a member at Oakhurst. He grew up in a missionary family in the Philippines, then went to college and gave up on the church. Then, he says, he "got politics," and realized that his church—"white middle-class born again evangelical"—was on the wrong side of justice issues. He became angry with the church and began staying away:

> But in 1994, when I ducked into the Oakhurst sanctuary, late—just for the sermon and a couple of hymns—once again, everything changed. Here was a church which was on the right side of all the issues of my good liberal agenda. Imagine my consternation. After years of complaining about the church and enjoying a self-righteous life of non-commitment, here was a church that was actually doing everything I had always said the church should do. Gone was my iron-clad excuse for opting out of the obligations of church membership, for not getting involved, for not staking my life on my good liberal convictions and my revitalized understanding of the Gospel, for not putting my money where my mouth was . . . you get the picture.
>
> Well, this was truly upsetting. But my parents had raised me right—and

there was no getting out of this pickle without completely invalidating any sense of integrity which I might hope to claim for my life. It was clear—I had to sign on.

What does Oakhurst mean to me? Broadly, Oakhurst is a church fulfilling the call of the church, living its mission, incarnating the presence of Christ in the world, the city, the neighborhood: feed the hungry, clothe the naked, visit the prisoner; there is neither Jew nor Greek, slave nor free, male nor female . . . you hear it every Sunday. More personally, Oakhurst began healing my own relationship with the Church, by making it impossible for me to continue drifting on the fringe. It opened the possibility for me to draw a line in the sand and take up a stand in the world against the principalities and powers, by committing to church membership and accepting the responsibilities and obligations of my baptism vows. Oakhurst offered me a place to translate my convictions into a flesh and blood life, affecting my decisions and the commitment of my time and energy.[7]

This young white man just received his Ph.D. in theology and has found a whole new world opening up to him at Oakhurst. He was raised in the Philippines but in a sheltered missionary compound. He has known the power of race, and he shared a story about his first remembrance of the category of race. He had never been out of the Philippines until his family went on furlough when he was a small boy. On their way to the States, where they would raise funds for their work, they stopped in Hawaii. For all of his young life, his servants and those who waited on him had been Filipino. In Hawaii, he remembers seeing white women in those roles for the first time, and he was embarrassed for them. He felt that there was something wrong with the white women that they would stoop so low as to do work reserved for "colored" women. He would have a lot to learn about the power of race.

He has found a new hope and a new vision at Oakhurst, and he has brought many gifts to us, too. He is a tall person who once served as the trunk of Goliath in a skit, while one of our young Jamaican boys served as the head of Goliath. He has worked with our senior high youth to produce great and powerful Christmas pageants, including one reggae pageant in which he appeared as the Bob Marley angel. Out of his firm grounding in the faith in his family life, out of his seeking and longing to make that faith his own, he has come to us, both receiving and sharing gifts.

That affirmation of the search and the journey is one of our central emphases at Oakhurst. We recognize the need to take risks, to make decisions about faith and about God and about the God we know in Jesus Christ, but we also affirm that we do not have to give up our intellect, our bodies, or our questions in our risk taking. One of the places we encourage such seeking and questioning is in our Supper Club, a group of members and friends who read books and go to movies, plays, and concerts, then gather for a meal to discuss them. We meet in one another's homes, so we have the additional benefit of often being in the space of someone of another race. For many people who come to Oakhurst, such an occasion is often the first time that they have ever been in the home of a person of another racial classification.

The coordinator of our Supper Club is a long-time member and was the first black member of the church's choir. She has seen much in her years at Oakhurst:

> Just as I have struggled in my own personal life to overcome some painful experiences so has Oakhurst struggled to become the kind of church it is today. Through the years, I have felt the presence of your love. I have felt the Holy Spirit moving in this place and have witnessed the power of God breaking down the barriers of the world that once divided us.[8]

This member has known her share of struggles. She grew up in south Georgia as a light-skinned black woman whose heritage included a white man's blood. She is a survivor of breast cancer. Her first husband was an alcoholic, and her daughter was murdered. She was one of the few black teachers in the local county school system when she moved to this area. She has seen her share of troubles and is one of the anchors at Oakhurst. She has been a bridge between the established white leadership and the emerging black leadership, and she and her husband have been among our strongest supporters. She is able to use humor and a sincere spirit to help move obstacles that previously seemed unmovable.

As the coordinator of our Supper Club, she has produced many surprises for us. Early in 1995, we began reading a book called *Brothers* by Sylvester Monroe, about black boys growing up into manhood in Robert Taylor Homes in Chicago in the 1960s and 1970s. The author was one of those boys. Our coordinator found out that Mr. Monroe was a correspondent for *Time Magazine* who was based in Atlanta. She contacted him to see if he would meet with our group to discuss his book, and he indicated that he might be able to squeeze in an hour with us. When he came to talk with us, he was so fascinated by our group that he stayed several hours. He later spoke in worship and eventually did the article on us that appeared in *Time*[9]. It was great publicity for Oakhurst!

Other long-time supporters of Oakhurst include an older white couple who have watched most of their white friends leave the church but have chosen to stay. He has been a member since 1936, and she, since 1946. For almost twenty years, they counted the offerings from worship and Sunday school, and their operations went so smoothly that we have found it difficult to replace them since they retired. She also was our treasurer for twenty years. They serve as a bridge to the past yet speak of the future and seek to live in that future also. She was a part of our prayer group when it was all white and is now the only white participant.

Another retired white couple came to us from the mission field, most recently as part of our denomination's mission in Nicaragua. Here is part of a letter they wrote to us:

> We want to thank you for your vision, courage, and prophetic leadership at Oakhurst. One of our deepest anxieties about coming back to the U.S. to live was finding a church to worship in and be a part of. I fully expected to drop out of the established Presbyterian Church for lack of finding a place relevant to what is going on in the world. What a surprise and joy it is to find a church like Oakhurst.[10]

This couple has brought a great missionary zeal and spirit to Oakhurst. One directs one of our children's choirs and is a member of our Worship Committee. They are both members of our Peacemaking and Justice Committee, and he coordinates our shelter work. They have also provided wonderful advocacy for a refugee family from Nigeria—and they come regularly for Workdays! They continue to be highly involved in the work of presbytery.

As we shall see in chapter 7, our sermons during Black History Month usually have a strong impact. Nibs usually selects people who have fought for justice for black people and tells their stories in his sermons. We have received many notes of gratitude for these sermons. One of them thanked us for lifting up Black History Month. The author was a young black woman who worked in a mostly white law firm. She was saddened that there was no celebration of Black History at her firm but gladdened that her church lifted it up so strongly. Another note had these words:

> I am a few days late in writing this note to you, but I want you to know how much I enjoyed your sermon February 26 on Fannie Lou Hamer. Truly she was a great lady, and you have helped us to understand the importance of such a powerful person. Without a doubt she made a difference for all of us. I often tell people when they complain that one of us can make a difference and each of us has a responsibility to try. That is the reason Ms. Hamer was such a great lady.[11]

This note was written by a former mayor of Decatur, the first and only black mayor and first African American to be elected to the city commission. She grew up under segregation in rural Georgia and moved to the city as a young adult. There she raised a family and fought to open access for black people to many institutions, including the libraries, schools, and hospitals. In her struggles she was fierce, refusing to allow white folks in those institutions much room to wiggle. She welcomed white allies, however, and learned how to negotiate well in the system while retaining her edge. In a recent meeting at our church with white business owners who are part of the gentrification of the community, she made it clear that she would not allow her grandson to frequent their establishments because of their racism. It stung them, and they tried to dismiss her concern as irrational and anachronistic. She held her ground, however, letting them know that she knew more about the black experience of racism than they did. She has known her share of sorrow—she is also a breast cancer survivor, and she watched her talented daughter slowly die of a rare blood disease. We mourned the passing of her daughter at a powerful funeral at our church. It is in our life together that she experiences—and that she enriches—our interweaving of spirituality and justice without disparaging either one.

That combination of spirituality and justice brings many folks to our congregation. Some leave because they are uncomfortable with the "Jesus" part of our community—they were initially drawn to us because of our work for social justice. Some leave because they believe that our emphasis on justice dilutes the proclamation of the gospel of Jesus Christ. From our point of view, the proclamation of the gospel must include social justice, else we fall into the trap of proclaiming not Jesus but a social view and a social order in the world. For us, we can't stay in the work for social justice without being centered in Jesus. The work is simply too frustrating and too complex, and has too few immediate results. Without the spiritual center of Jesus, we would have burned up and burned out a long time ago. Here are words from one of our young white members who was struck by our weaving of spirituality and justice.

I first visited Oakhurst in 1996, a few weeks before the general election in November. What impressed me were Nibs' remarks during the time for "joys and concerns," in which he stated the importance of voting. As odd as it seems, I had never before heard a church representative, during worship, speak in this way. I had heard those from the Christian right in previous years advocate votes for Ronald Reagan and anti-abortion candidates. In the opposite vein, I had attended chapel services at a nearby theological school during which it would have been difficult, judging from the liturgy, to determine in what city or country—not to mention on which planet—one was located at that particular moment.

But I was genuinely surprised, and pleased, to hear advocacy for the simple citizen sacrament of voting. Nibs' statements on that day were consistent with the congregation's view that God attends to the so-called profane events, those everyday moments that occur during the 166 hours (or thereabouts) per week that one is not in church. "Seek the welfare of the city where I have sent you into exile," writes Jeremiah, "and pray to the Lord on its behalf, for in its welfare you will find your welfare" (29:7, NRSV).[12]

He is the coordinator of our tutoring program, a member of our building and grounds committee, and a free-lance editor. He brings great energy and vision to Oakhurst, and he has found a place where spirituality and justice can be put in the same sentence. In addition to all this, he is a Sunday school teacher for our junior high group. Last year he took them to an exhibit of Gordon Parks's photographs at Emory's Carlos Museum, where they received a tour led by the director of education for the museum, who is also an Oakhurst member. One of the great benefits of that trip for our community of faith was a series of bulletin covers, using Parks's photographs and the young people's interpretation of the meaning of the text of Psalm 121.

Not all of our members have formal degrees or cross easily the boundaries into higher education. One of our matriarchs is a person of African American and Cherokee heritage, a mother of ten children, and a grandmother of many more. She is raising three of her grandchildren who were abandoned by a daughter addicted to drugs. Although she has little formal education, she is vitally educated in spiritual matters and in matters of the heart. Her impact at Oakhurst is described by another member:

On one of my first Sundays at Oakhurst, an "older" African-American woman asked the pastor if she could share a song with the congregation during the time of "Sharing of Joys and Concerns." She walked to the front and sang in strong voice a song which she said the Lord had sent to her the evening before. The congregation was still and quiet as they listened to the very real words of prayer which were sung from this woman's mouth.

She is one of the many reasons I chose to attend Oakhurst church. On my first Sunday at Oakhurst, I felt that I had "come home." There are no words which can fully describe the power and fellowship of prayer at Oakhurst Church. Personally, I can only describe the emotion.

My experience with prayer in the Presbyterian Church was a very traditional one. Growing up in a white Presbyterian church, prayer was silent and orderly. Prayer had focus and direction. Prayer was dignified and careful.

Her prayer was not silent or orderly. It was not focused or directed at a particular aim. Although it was dignified, it was not careful. Her prayer to the Lord was a testimony of her faith and belief in a God who had not ever left her side. As she sang, the power of her prayer brought the community of Oakhurst together as one people—listening to her song and truly feeling the presence of the Lord. I had never before experienced such an emotion.[13]

This matriarch's prayer is so powerful because she needs God so much in her life to sustain her day by day. She is not ashamed of expressing her need for God, and her faith in God's daily providence touches many of us middle-class folk—black and white alike—who try to fool ourselves into believing that we don't really *need* God on a daily basis. Every now and then a crisis may force us into the foxhole where we utter a desperate cry to God, but the point of middle-class life is to convince ourselves that we are moving towards self-sufficiency, independence, and control. Her prayer and her praise of God speak to us about the realities of life and the necessity of daily dependence on God.

That sense of dependence on God is a powerful part of our life together at Oakhurst. We emphasize it as the truth of our lives, not in a moaning, disparaging way but in a celebrating, affirming way. Dependence is often the key that unlocks the doors of our hearts to God, to others, and to ourselves. Though in a culture like ours, which sees dependence as a weakness, we fight and often seek to deny it, the idea of dependence often brings us home. Many of our members have known that journey. After a devastating accident, one woman began searching for a new church:

> I realized that it was the spiritual side of my life that was missing. I tried attending several different types of churches, but as a former Roman Catholic the concept of "church shopping" was completely foreign to me. Luckily, I met John Carson and Caroline Leach at a community meeting in Decatur, and they of course talked about Oakhurst. I was intrigued, and started attending services. What I found was acceptance, diversity, and people committed both to each other and to their deep and abiding faith—a faith that I am just beginning to understand. As Nibs reminds us every week, we have made a mess of many things in this world, but at Oakhurst we continue to seek discernment, and continue to ask the tough questions about who we are as a community. It is that questioning and that faith that draws so many of us to Oakhurst.[14]

This member has been a powerful witness in our community and in our church. She has been the point person to redevelop a parcel of land that will include affordable housing in our community, and she has been caught between those who believe that money is the key to life and those who believe that there is a different key. As we indicated earlier, our community is struggling through gentrification, and many young white people moving into the community believe in meritocracy, the idea that you get what you earn and you earn what you get. Many of them have expressed their discomfort about this nonprofit organization providing affordable housing in our community because it might stem the tide of rapidly escalating property values. She has brought these concerns and her struggle in the midst of them to our monthly worship services for wholeness and healing. This worship service is an informal time when a small group gathers to share their pain and their longing for healing and reconciliation. The idea of healing is not so much to rid ourselves of the disease or the pain but to regain a sense that God is at the center of our lives, a sense that is often greatly disturbed and even shattered by disease or tragic happenings in our lives.

In our life together, we seek to provide space for people to share their anger and disappointment in God, emotions that are often triggered by accidents and diseases that attack us. Again, our emphasis is that God wants that side of ourselves also, because God wants our passion, not our perfection. And our passion is connected to those deep parts of ourselves where anxiety and hope dwell side by side, sometimes intertwined with one another. Our emphasis is that these emotions and these questions are not indicators of faithlessness but rather just the opposite: signs of a deep and longing faith in a benevolent, loving Parent who allows and even welcomes those difficult questions of "Why, God, Why?"

One of our families experienced this interweaving of anxiety and hope a couple of years ago when the husband had a terrible fall from a ladder and was in a coma for days, not expected to live. If he did live, he would have severe brain damage and likely could not function at all. This white couple were former missionaries who brought gifts to us but who also came to us because they realized that, after working many years with people in Africa, they actually knew very little about people of African descent. In response to his accident, our church—and many other churches because of their missionary connections—went into round-the-clock care, prayer, and vigils. In an astonishing miracle, the husband regained consciousness and began to heal. He did sustain some brain damage but has returned to about 90 percent of his capacity. They were both welcomed back into worship with a standing ovation, as we celebrated his recovery as well as her loving care for him, for she had experienced a frustrating and difficult transition. It has been and continues to be a long journey, but they have found a place where they are not only accepted but welcomed and celebrated, as she writes,

> After the Christmas pageant—long after the pageant on Sunday night, I said to Bob, "Are you about ready to leave?" (We were still standing in the sanctuary). And he replied, "I don't think I'll ever want to leave this place."

Thank you for providing the leadership which makes Oakhurst the loving and accepting place that it is—for all of us![15]

This couple had earlier been part of the revival of our youth program at Oakhurst. After a long absence of young people, we had a budding and mixed group of black and white middle school youth, including our son. After talking with several leaders, our Christian Education Committee asked this retired missionary couple to be the youth leaders. They were hesitant because of their age, their whiteness, and their lack of knowledge of black people. Yet their missionary zeal kicked in, and they heard the request for what we took it to be: a calling from God. They agreed to do it for a year. It was a bold and difficult step. Some of our strong black leaders came to us and asked us how we could have white adults leading black youth. While acknowledging the importance of their question, we answered their difficult point with a simple reply: Who else would do it? We knew that this couple was responsible, diligent, creative, and willing to try, and no black folk had agreed to do it. We all reluctantly agreed that it was the best that we could do at the moment. God blessed us tremendously through this youth group and its leaders, and we want to share brief glimpses of five of these youth as evidence of God's movement.

One of the African American girls in the group was the daughter of a woman who raised concerns about the white leadership. Despite her concerns, the mother insisted on her daughter's participation in the group. This young girl grew to love the white leaders in a way that astonished and warmed us all and that gave testimony to God's power to break down barriers. As she has grown into a young woman, she has retained a strong black consciousness but has seen and has experienced that race is not the final word in our lives. As she goes through her journey in college, she has retained close ties with us.

Another of the African American girls came to us through her friends rather than through her family, which was not part of our church. This young girl lived in a dangerous situation in which drugs were sold out of her house, and there were always men around looking for drugs and more. Because of this situation, she had begun to withdraw into herself for protection, and in so doing, she had little confidence in her ability to navigate out in the world. In order to survive, she hoped not to be noticed. Our leaders helped her build her confidence, find a new place to stay, and hear a new definition of herself as daughter of God. She has blossomed under this care, is now in nursing school, and feels that she has a life after all.

An African American boy came to the church with his family, and he and Bob, the male leader, quickly developed a bond, starting with sports but moving out into other areas. This boy became a football player in junior high and high school, and our leaders went to as many of his games as possible, often encouraging other members to go along. This young man is attending college on a football scholarship, and, after Bob's fall from the ladder, he became an instrumental part of Bob's recovery, working with him over a summer as he struggled to recover some of his building skills that seemed to have been scrambled by the brain damage from the fall.

A white boy involved in the youth group was our son, David. He was three years old when we came to Oakhurst and has grown through adolescence into manhood there. Finding himself to be the only white boy in the group, he went out and recruited other white boys. One stayed and has become his close friend. David has received many gifts from Oakhurst, and we became aware of some of them as he began to decide on colleges. He was strongly attracted to Davidson College, a small Presbyterian liberal arts school near Charlotte, North Carolina. Nibs tried to discourage him for many reasons, including the cost of going there. Assuming that he would get a viable financial aid package, Nibs pointed out that Davidson was conservative and even looked like the old line about who Presbyterians really were: the Republican party at prayer. David replied, "Dad, I've grown up knowing all kinds of different people at Oakhurst. Don't you think I can deal with Republicans at Davidson?" And so he has. He has gone to Davidson and has blossomed there, drawing from insights that he learned from our youth group.

Our final youth profile is an African American girl who has had a profound effect on our church. She and her three younger sisters came to Oakhurst with their parents, and she became part of our youth group. She was a talented and vivacious girl who easily took leadership in the group. We feared trouble in their home life, however, for we perceived the mother as being dominated by her third husband, who was also the girl's father figure. With our roots in the women's movement, we began to encourage the mother to come out and stand up for herself. The husband began to get the message that we saw him as just another black man who was insensitive to women and wanted to dominate his wife.

Things got worse, and finally the mother went out on the streets on drugs. As pastors, we were certain that the husband was the culprit—that he had gotten the wife hooked on drugs and that this drug dependence had caused her to abandon her family. One of our black members confronted us, however, indicating that our racism was clear, that we had completely missed the dynamics because we had allowed ourselves to believe what society says about black men. She suggested that our "white savior" complex had kicked in for this situation. She was right. It turned out that this was the latest episode of the mother's long struggle with drug addiction, and the husband had been holding the family together.

The girl in our youth group had also been holding the family together, serving as the mother figure for her three younger sisters. The black member who had confronted us then suggested a bold move: she would take this girl and the next oldest into her home and serve as a mother figure for them if the church would provide backup support. The call went out through the membership, and offers of time, rides, and money poured in. This girl could have some time when she could be nurtured rather than being only the nurturer, and the combination of our member's home and nurture and our congregation's support of this journey worked. She has grown into a young woman and has been supported financially and spiritually by our membership throughout her college career in North Carolina. This is what she said about our involvement in her life in a sermon that she gave at her college:

> I continue to be amazed at the power of God, seeing how he brought me to where I am from a background that seemed desolate. To say that my family was poor would probably be an understatement. My family struggled with alcohol and drug problems and limited education opportunities among others. Although I fought to focus on my education, I was often distracted by such problems. I was compelled to take on the role of holding my family together for quite some time. (I'm still trying to figure out how I made that babysitting money stretch. That's a biblical miracle in itself.)
>
> The situation gradually became worse. Just when I knew I couldn't take it anymore, God stepped in to deliver me. He sent his angels to walk me through these troubles. These earthly angels came in the form of my church family. Not only did Oakhurst step in to provide the much-needed financial assistance, but its members also provided me with guidance, emotional support, and a renewed faith in God. My guardian also emerged from this group of angels. Till this day, God is still using these angels to watch over me.[16]

It is this ability to cross all kinds of boundaries—to make mistakes in doing so, to be challenged and engaged by others in those mistakes, to grow together in the process—that attracts so many different kinds of people to Oakhurst. We are gaining a lot of young white members, and here are the reflections of one of them:

> After our first visit at Oakhurst, I was intrigued. This church went against so many of my misconceptions about the South. The diversity of the congregation was amazing to me. And when we were visited in our home (all the way out in Snellville!) by Nibs, and later Inez, we knew this was a special place—a place where people went out of their way to be welcoming.
>
> Five years later, I've learned a lot from Oakhurst. Moreover, the experience has humbled me. This congregation operates more like a family than

probably any other I've experienced—we laugh together, cry together, and, of course, occasionally get irritated with one another. And I've seen members of our congregation give of themselves in extraordinary ways. Finally, Oakhurst is confrontational—it doesn't allow me to be complacent or to ignore the injustices and inequities of this imperfect world of ours.

I've still got a lot to learn from this place—and maybe that's what I love most about Oakhurst.[17]

This reflection is a from a young woman who, along with her husband, has shown exceptional leadership and skills in our midst. They have helped us to develop a strong committee on peacemaking and justice, and he has been instrumental in bringing us into the electronic age, though Nibs comes screaming and kicking. It is a sign of our aging as pastors that we thought they were teenagers just out of high school when they first came to Oakhurst. He has a doctorate in biology, and she is working on her doctorate in chemistry.

Some of our members do not have college degrees or advanced degrees. One of the pillars of our church has the authority of a matriarch but isn't old enough to be called by that title! She is an African American woman who has been a member here for over twenty years. Her children have grown up here, and she has buried many of her family members here—her husband, her mother, two brothers. She has been a great support to us. In the early days of our ministry at Oakhurst when there were powerful conflicts because we sought to make so many changes, she was a source of hope and encouragement, and she was a good translator to some white members who were upset with the changes. Because of her personality and her reliability, she has always been trusted by both black and white members of Oakhurst. She was essential in getting our gospel choir started, and she is a fierce witness for justice. She has received death threats at work for her emphasis on racial justice, and she once took on the district attorney of our county at a meeting at our church over his decision to try a thirteen-year-old black boy as an adult for theft of a pair of sneakers.[18] Nibs remembers well her gentle insistence as he was approached during his first black funeral. Seeing his nervousness, she asked him, "You've never done a black funeral, have you?" Relieved that it was out in the open, he replied that he had not, and she gave him a quick course on the differences between black funerals and white funerals—another translation showing us the way.

Other members at Oakhurst prefer to stay behind the scenes but also do a huge amount of work. One such member is the light-skinned black woman whom Nibs mistook for being white when she came to hear him preach in Nashville. She has been a constant at Oakhurst, easily able to go between several of the cultures in our community of faith. She was born in Mississippi and grew up in Chicago, part of that great migration of black people who left the oppression of the South for the land of milk and honey in the North.[19] She is the "secretary" of our weekly prayer group, writing down the concerns and joys as they are shared in Sunday worship, then lifting them up at our prayer meeting a couple of days later. She is a great cook and uses those skills to minister to many of us as individuals and as we gather as a community. She has been a strong supporter of our shift to a multicultural church, and because so many people trust her, she has been a valuable translator.

There are many other members who are an important part of this life in multicultural ministry. Indeed, the presence of all our members enables us to seek to live as the people of God. Space prevents us from profiling additional members, but we do want to lift up one more. She is a black woman who has been an invaluable translator and visionary for us. She brings the unusual quality of being open and frank with white folks while always giving white people space to experience and to demonstrate their humanity. For us as pastors, she has been an entry point into black life in a manner that we rarely experience: as a helpful translator in the trenches of the tensions between the black experience and the culture of gay and lesbian people. She has also been a steady guide and challenger for white people as we stumble through the minefield of our own racism in our desire to "fix" the lives of black people. In a remarkable way she has been fiercely loyal to her African American heritage while inviting white people into her life and into life together at Oakhurst. The result is deepening insight and growing faith and a belief that this entire work is done by the commissioning of the Holy Spirit, as she likes to put it.

Our life together *is* the commissioning of the Holy Spirit. We have crossed the gulf of the great racial divide with much stumbling and bumbling and heartache, yet, in crossing it, we have been graced with glimpses of the Promised Land. Oakhurst is a place not where everyone and their heritage is homogenized but rather where difference—diversity—is affirmed, celebrated, and woven into the tapestry of the people of God. In this meaning, we have discovered the importance of being in one another's presence. We will explore the idea of presence more in chapter 8, but for now, we note that it is the day-to-day working, worshiping, caring, confronting, and loving one another that has given us a glimpse of the new reality that Jesus brought to us: a whole new world, a world more celebrated and celebrating, a world more complex yet simpler, a world more grace-filled than we ever imagined possible. It is the work of the Holy Spirit. Who are these people? We are people who have been blessed to be pioneers in new space and new place. We understand well the mighty acts of God. We are one of them. We are part of that great heritage of Pentecost people.

Chapter Seven

Seasons of Celebration: The Details of Multicultural Ministry

With a mixture of planned action and spontaneity at work in each event in the congregation, the outcome is really unknown. People enter into the experience with anticipation that something exciting and something good is unfolding, but with little control over the final product. We heard the choir sing "There's a Sweet, Sweet, Spirit in This Place" repeatedly as its introit; the people of this church have come to trust that spirit.

—Charles R. Foster and Theodore Brelsford[1]

Make a joyful noise to the Lord, all the earth. Worship the Lord with gladness, come into God's presence with singing!

—Psalm 100:1–2

Blessed is the king who comes in the name of the Lord! Peace in heaven, and glory in the highest heaven!

—Luke 19:38

Education in the multiethnic church moves between the joyful noise encouraged in Psalm 100 to the enthusiasm of the great parade of Palm Sunday. We expect the Holy Spirit to breathe new life into every activity. Our operating norm is that there are no problems, only possibilities. We deeply believe that the Holy Spirit works when we are opened to new possibilities enriched by the central traditions given to us in the Protestant Reformation of education and worship. Our hope is to recover the wonder and majesty of God and to recover the excitement of knowing God's love in our lives. In this sense, we are all asked to return to the excitement and curiosity of being children.

Let the little children come to me, and do not stop them; for it is to such as these that the kingdom of God belongs. Truly I tell you, whoever does not receive the kingdom of God as a little child will never enter it. (Luke 18:15–17)

How does it work, and can I do it in my church? These are questions that are asked of us, most often right after people say, "We could never do that here!" The world that our church missionaries to other countries brought home to us in our youth is now at our doorstep in the United States. Folks taught and trained by missionaries to those strange "foreign lands" are now living and working in the United States. As pastors we had never had a multiethnic church situation before. In the early years, few printed resources that addressed multicultural situations were available for the church school programs or worship services. We began by searching libraries for information about the ethnic groups that formed our congregation. And we learned to ask questions of our members, especially those who taught in our schools. We broke the rules by coloring in faces on pictures that had been sent with curricula, and redrawing pictures that children would be coloring. We gave away from the church library books and resources that did not reflect the many colors of our congregation. We looked wide and deliberately for books, resources, visual art, and music that reflected those whom God sent to Oakhurst.

We asked questions and more questions. How did you celebrate Christmas at your home or your country of birth? What was special about Easter where you grew up? What are the memorable celebrations of your home church? The answers to these questions are important for developing the seasons of celebrations in a multiethnic church. Asking questions can lead to a treasure trove of information that can be used in educating the entire congregation about all the children of God's great world. It can also be a reminder of how our personal assumptions are often barriers and how our particular upbringing can offer only a small glimpse into the world that God created.

To imagine ourselves as learners rather than experts enables church leadership to cherish what is available within a congregation, whether large or small. We also learned to value resources available at bookstores, school supply stores, and libraries. Children's sections of bookstores now have an abundance of stories from different lands that highlight celebrations special in a particular culture—celebrations that can enhance our own traditional ones. Asia has a delightful "Children's Day" about the same time that we celebrate Easter Tide on our church calendar. Kites are the order of the day. We write messages of endearment on kites that are shared with our church families during worship or at the greeting time on the church lawn after worship.

Decorations of children's art work are used as often as possible in our sanctuary as well as in the fellowship hall. Each season brings new opportunities for expression of God's love of children around the world. Children's art is important to our worship. Their visual art is not hidden in their rooms but brought into the sanctuary as their gifts. For example, each year for Pentecost we select a simple ornament for the children to make and hang them in our sanctuary windows—all sixteen of them! We have used kites from Asia, colorful piñatas from Latin America, and flags representing the different countries of our church members. We have also had stars from the Middle East, paper lanterns from Latin America, doves from Japan, and butterflies from Jamaica—the latter with red, yellow, and orange streamers blowing in the breeze coming from our open windows.

All artists in every medium are encouraged to bring into Oakhurst their gifts of color and imagination. We are all enriched in this exercise. We have designed new Advent banners that give us the visual image of our many colors: the infant Jesus has a face that is creatively divided between tan and black. The Wise Leaders are of different ethnic groups, and the shepherds are joyfully multicolored as well. Easter banners have multicolored angels and astonished disciples from many nations.

One of our artists, who was raised on the mission field in Mozambique, has brought our Advent countries to life. For each of the past four years, she has painted on large cardboard boxes the faces of those who live in the region of interest: singers in Latin America, dancers from Senegal, the Holy Family from Africa and Jamaica. Animals and flowers from these countries come alive with rich colors in their shapes. Butterflies on the islands of Jamaica are bright and bold; flowers of Latin America add color to door frames; stars in the night sky of Africa all light up our fellowship hall as they hang from the ceiling. Last year we dressed large puppets from Appalachia in the clothes of African Americans who ran from slavery to hide in freedom in the mountains and in the clothes of Europeans who traveled from Ireland and Scotland with new hope. Our Holy Family were the Native Americans who lived and loved the land for two thousand years before they were forced to leave. Everyone, young and old, enjoyed coloring the stars based on quilt patterns found in the traditions of Africans, Europeans, and Native Americans.

When the day of Pentecost had come, they were all together in one place. And suddenly from heaven there came a sound like the rush of a violent wind, and it filled the entire house where they were sitting. (Acts 2:1)

Embracing the differences in a congregation can be the source of "new wine." That is the most difficult idea for any congregation to accept while at the same time honoring traditional ways of learning and worship. Yet the first church at Pentecost was born during a Jewish celebration in the city that was at the very heart of the Jewish faith. When the followers of Jesus shared the Good News in the different languages of all who gathered, many wanted to join in this new fellowship rather than run away. They heard in a real way that God was calling their names and seeking their energy and commitment for a new beginning.

A central question for us at Oakhurst was, What understanding of faith would bind us as we traveled together as children of God? The great mystery was answered with the most obvious. Oakhurst follows the seasons of the church year for our education programs and worship planning. The seasons of Advent, Epiphany, Lent and Easter, and Pentecost became the common ground that centers our celebrations together. Following the seasons of the church year is a useful place to begin. However, sticking to lectionary readings from the Bible became too confining, though we do use them sometimes during the year. The seasons of the church year offer boundaries but with numerous opportunities to include more of a particular season from other ethnic traditions.

We will now take you on a journey through some of our seasonal celebrations. On this journey you will see our insights and our mistakes—and remember, one of the great gifts of multicultural churches is that the possibilities are almost endless!

Advent

Advent is a great time in the church year. Everyone seems to be in a good mood and excited about the coming season of celebration. The story of a family receiving the Christ child is familiar yet offers an opportunity to try new ideas within the old, old story. We began in the early years of our ministry by honoring the traditions Oakhurst already had in place. When we came, the church members were discouraged and the building was dreary. There was a solid core of adults but only a few older children, and only forty people attending worship. Our own children were three years and four months old! They became the nursery class.

The church had, in fact, not done much celebrating of Advent in several years. In looking for decorations from the past, we found faded plastic poinsettias and dusty glass candle globes. The one available banner was wrinkled and torn. We began by slowly trading old plastic for new, sweet smelling greenery from members' yards. In the coming years, as the spirits of the congregation rose, we were more deliberate to add meaningful decorations as well as worship services for this special season. We also began an Advent team approach in coordinating all education and worship activities. Advent themes are often suggested by the pastors but are also suggested by members. Themes for the next year's Advent often come as we prepare and celebrate the current year. We have learned to make notes as ideas come to us. The new list for next year has already started! If music from other traditions is involved, we try to work with the choir directors and the organist beginning in the early summer months.

Our worship, Sunday school classes, and seasonal activities began to explore the many dimensions of the Christmas story—the surprise of an infant born to a teenage mother pregnant before marriage, an old couple having a baby, smelly shepherds, and wise leaders who follow stars. All of these characters are those that God uses to tell of the coming of God among us at Advent. To seek a new surprise from God has brought delight to us each year. Imagine being asked by members what is in store for next year as the decorations begin to come down following Epiphany Sunday!

Finding resources are as near as the first person on the first pew. Each year we begin with a theme. One year we explored the theme of covenant couples: Abraham and Sarah, Ruth and Boaz, Elizabeth and Zachariah, and Mary and Joseph. One of the most interesting series to preach and teach is the Genealogy of Jesus found in Matthew. We pick four or more of the foreparents of Jesus and preach about them. We began Advent one year by hanging up paper skeletons found around the Halloween season. Hanging these on the wall behind the pulpit, we used them to speak about the skeletons found in Jesus' closet, about how God uses people we would consider ordinary and outsiders to bring the Good News of Christmas then and now. For example, four women who might cause embarrassment to us but are in fact listed as the foremothers of Jesus, the Christ, are Tamar, Rahab, Ruth, and the "wife of Uriah" (Bathsheba). We have also used this same genealogy to preach on the unusual names mentioned: Aminadab, Salmon, Rehoboam, Jehoshaphat, and the rest. Some of these men mentioned have their own challenging stories. God's grace is made very evident through these foreparents.

Another theme is to search for the "signs" used in the Christmas story, such as stars or angels. We chose angels from the Christmas story one year, and we found that there are major differences between these messengers that God sends and the popular notions of today. Another year we researched the legends of the wise leaders and of plants and animals. We found many interesting legends that can be used in Children's Time, sermons, and the pageant. The middle-school group that year wore tie-dyed pillow cases and wrote a poem using the plant legends. The younger children made animal masks and sang their stories. There is a rich tradition of the wise leaders from Ethiopia that is much older than the one we usually know. Do you know their Ethiopian names? Did you know that the three cornered hat the Ethiopian kings wore was made popular during the French Revolution and is worn by George Washington in the crossing at the Delaware River!

The colors of Christmas also offer possibilities for teachings during Advent. Green, for example, was used by Europeans to decorate in the dark, cold winter months to chase away the evil spirits. We know that Martin Luther found a tree glistening with starlight so he chopped it down and brought it home for his family! He also used German folk music with new words to sing the Christmas story for the "new church" of the Reformation. Since we have an abundance of kudzu around the South, our youth cut and wove our Advent wreath that we decorate every year to show that God brings beauty even to the ugly kudzu wreath. Green is very alive in the countries of our nearest neighbors—Latin and Central America and the Caribbean islands—during our cold winter months. We find it ironic that the poinsettias grow wild in the warm climates but are usually pictured with snow-capped holly and ivy!

Time with Children during the worship service is a good time to begin the process of sharing other ethnic traditions or holidays that are held during the Christmas season. Jewish and Muslim holidays coincide with our own. Some folks can enjoy the children's response and not realize that they are learning something new as well. We also invite our professional educators because they are our best storytellers. Though they are our ambassadors every day, they are happy to share with the children during these few minutes, especially during holidays. Oakhurst is blessed with a diverse group of educators, active and retired, who bring many resources from their work.

For the past four years we have explored the countries of origin of our church members. We began when our denomination was using the Year with Latin Americans as an emphasis (1996–1997). We had former missionaries from Mexico and Nicaragua as well as those who were born, worked, or visited in South, Central, and Latin America. The new *Presbyterian Hymnal* had also just come out, so we were blessed with music from these countries. Yes, we learned to sing in Spanish! The poinsettia and its legends come from Latin America, as do some great stories of donkeys. In a trialogue sermon, we told the story of Juan Diego encountering the Lady of Guadalupe, and, of course, Nibs got to be the donkey! We now try each year to find at least one donkey story just for him.

We also began a tradition that has continued as we work with our senior high youth group. Along with their adult advisors, these youth write and produce the annual Christmas pageant. In the Year with Latin Americans the students used the traditional posada parade but spoke it in rap form. A banker, military person, doctor, and others spoke in rap verse of having no room in their homes. Finally, an old shed in back of a hotel became the stable for the birth of Jesus. Everyone who had ethnic clothes from any country wore them and entered into the parade. Our youth have written and produced many profound tellings of the Christmas stories. One year the shepherds were the zoo keepers at our local zoo, and Jesus was born near a downtown playground. Among the shepherds were two boys whose families were from Mexico. When the angels, dressed in suit jackets, appeared with bright lights to tell of the great, good news, these shepherds took out their sunglasses!

We have added the countries of Africa, the islands of the Caribbean, and the region of Appalachia in our most recent Advent themes. Our families from other countries are excited to share the memories of celebrations in their own traditions. At the Christmas pageant, we encourage folks to wear their ethnic clothes and bring special traditional foods for us to share at our dinner before the pageant. There are people in every congregation who have lived or traveled in other countries, and the folks at Oakhurst now know to bring back items of interest to share with all of us when they visit another country. During our study of Appalachia we hung family quilts all over the sanctuary as part of our decoration theme. All ethnic groups in America have quilts, including Native Americans, African Americans, and European Americans. Our artist drew stars for us to color, reflecting the images of our three groups, but put in a quilt outline. Often those who come dressed in ethnic clothing are asked to bring in the gifts as the wise leaders as they come to honor Emmanuel, God with us. We lift up the history, leaders, and gifts that each of these peoples have given to us as world citizens.

Kwanzaa

We also have included the celebrations of Kwanzaa in our worship. We began six years ago with a series of Advent sermons using the seven principles of Kwanzaa. We were reminded during this series of the many gifts our African American members bring to us in their strength and faithfulness in the long struggle for freedom. Kwanzaa began with a search by Maulana Karenga in 1966 to bring together his African heritage and his American history. Kwanzaa means "the first" and begins on December 26 each year. During our pageant that first year, we began the service with our younger youth dancing a welcome dance from Nigeria. These youth participate in the African dance class in our community recreation center. We asked our community leaders to each bring a "gift of leadership" to share with all of us. Each gift was wrapped in a streamer that had one of the Kwanzaa principles spelled out. Each streamer was presented and hung on a banner under the sign of the dove descending.

The year following the Year with Latin Americans, we studied Africa and the earliest history of the church in Africa. We sang in the African languages and learned of the bravery of its leaders as we explored the Christmas story. The youth and youth leaders in this season wrote, produced, and acted in a play, using the Lion King characters from the Disney movie but with a twist. Told with the animated faces of the central characters enlarged as puppets, the seekers were following a bright African star in search of the real king. The African drumming group that practiced in our church provided the rhythmic background and had us all dancing and clapping by the end of the evening. The dinner before the service also featured foods from Africa.

World Communion Sunday

The Protestant Reformation gave the church the greatest gift for our multi-ethnic churches. The reformers believed that the church belongs to all the people and that God's gifts of ministries are in all people. The expectation that the Holy Spirit is at work in and through us is what the Risen Jesus left with us. Jesus tells Mary in the garden, "Do not hold me." We are the witnesses of Christ in our day. The Table of our Lord is a table of welcome, not exclusion. Our church family includes many different ethnic traditions and educational levels. We seek to honor them, not blend them together so there is no meaning for anyone.

On World Communion Sunday, and indeed every time we celebrate the Lord's Supper, we are surrounded by the world. On this special Sunday in October we bring breads that represent each of the ethnic groups in our church. Our table is full! After church, in the fellowship hall, we all taste these breads from many nations.

Easter Sunday

Easter Sunday is an array of flowers and festivities. Easter is the most celebrated Christian day in most countries, with days of preparation for family gatherings and special care in decorating with flowers. We have adopted from Latin America the idea of decorating an empty cross with flowers on Easter Sunday. During the Sunday school time, we tell each class, as they come to decorate, the story of Holy Week and what makes this day special. Before worship begins, children are at the front of the sanctuary helping adults who enter put flowers in the cross that will be carried in at the beginning of the Easter service. We add youthful dancers as disciples, telling the good news of the resurrection. All the Easter banners are up, and the church is full of celebration noise!

Angels

We chose the angel messengers one year because angels were just then becoming popular. We began where we always begin at Advent: with questions. Who were these angels, and how did God use them to tell the story of faith? We gained many unexpected insights. For example, angels in the Bible are often people, with an occasional appearance by Gabriel and the heavenly hosts. As often as we have read and reread the stories since we were children, we were once again struck with an insight that has helped us in continuing the journey at Oakhurst. With every entrance into a person's life, the angel begins with "Do Not Be Afraid"! God's work goes in unexpected ways, and God is with us as we seek to be witnesses in our community of worship, even when the way is not easy or clear.

We were very moved by those comforting words from God's messengers. The message from God that the angels delivered was a task that challenged the recipient to become a new person. Think about the stories of a teenage Mary, a distraught Joseph, and the smelly shepherds. Their lives were never the same. The multiethnic church brings both fear and fire but is never dull.

Signs, Symbols, and Art

Symbols and signs have become very important to us over the years. For example, we are certainly more sensitive to the use of color, with the many hues of folks of our congregation. Many grow up hearing that Jesus brought light into the dark world—that light shines in darkness, that the world was full of sin and darkness covered the world. Using these images in this way implies that black is bad and white is good. One of the first ways this connotation hit us was during the time we preached on the colors of Advent. The color "White" is prominent in the decorations of the Christmas season— white can symbolize purity, thus pushing the color black to represent sin. We decided to work with the color red instead because everyone has red blood, and the live poinsettias were all over the pulpit area for the first time. We are reminded to avoid implying that all darkness is bad as we look into the faces of African, African American, and Caribbean children, whose lives are often complicated because of negative images of themselves based on the color of their skin.

The imaging of being multiethnic is very important. We spent the first years storing and "losing" pictures, books, and curricula that no longer looked like our flower garden of colors. We continually seek out artists and others who can add to our growing collection of banners, books, and resources that reflect our congregation and the world that is ours today. Black History Month finds walls adorned with pictures of African kings and queens, African American inventors, educators, church leaders, and other leaders—including our own members. During the worship services in February, we preach about those who have helped to make our nation a more just place to live for everyone.

Appliance boxes can be transformed into an array of visual art. We look forward every year to working with one of the artists who was born and raised in Mozambique. She brings in ideas and creates beautiful images, such as wise men riding in a Jitney bus, Senegal dancers as angels, and nativity scenes of Masai, Hispanic people, and Native Americans. We do not have financial resources to pay artists, so we invite everyone to bring knowledge and enthusiasm to work during our decorating times. Our use of material resources would make anyone concerned with recycling proud! Ideas produce more ideas, and each one feels they can add a bit more until we think we are really in another space. God does richly bless those who seek!

Curriculum

We are often looking for newer resources to compliment the church curriculum that is available. We value the time and commitment that the denominational staff has put into providing quality curricula for all ages. We are fortunate today that school supply stores and book stores, especially those with multiethnic emphasis, now carry an abundance of cultural resources that can be adapted for church education. Caroline visits them frequently. National church offices are developing more materials that are helpful in enhancing God's Word with art, music, and educational resources.

Martin Luther King Jr.'s Birthday

January finds us in a special place in the seasons of the church. The search for stars and the gifts of wise leaders who risked their lives in Epiphany is important for us to share. Many of our folk have tasted the bitter fruit of racism, sexism, homophobia, and painful differences in values. Our families come in many different configurations from all areas of our country and the world. We cherish this month and seek anew our own courage to follow the dream and learn from the dreamers. Dr. Martin Luther King Jr. holds a special place in our hearts at Oakhurst, for we live in the metro Atlanta area, and many of our folk worked with Dr. King. Oakhurst is made up of folk who seek his vision of the "beloved community." We begin his birthday celebration just as he did in years past: with a breakfast—our folk who know and can cook a traditional breakfast of eggs and grits begin early that morning. Each year we seek to find renewed meaning in Dr. King's dream. In 2000, we gathered all those in our church who knew and worked with Dr. King for a storytelling event and had a grand morning of remembering as we moved into the new millennium. Powerful stories they were, and we remain grateful for each storyteller's witness to the continuing struggle and his or her commitment to being a part of the "beloved community" of Oakhurst. This past year we had each table read a quote from a speech of Dr. King and then draw, write, or tell in their own words what the quote meant to them. Children, youth, and adults all took the stage with thoughtful reflections to share.

Black History Month

In 1988, we decided to emphasize Black History Month by focusing on particular people in American history in our sermons. We encountered resistance from some members because Black History Month is a secular remembrance and because the devotion of an entire month to Black History would guarantee that the power of racism and the deletion of the history of African Americans would be highlighted and noted. Our response was that half of our membership was black and that we needed to lift up and celebrate their history in a manner that is usually ignored.

We both love history, so this was not a stretch or a chore for us. Nibs was especially inspired by encountering the life of Ida B. Wells, a woman born in slavery who matured to be the leading opponent of lynching and one of the fiercest fighters for equality for black people and for women in American history.[2] The more he learned about her life, the more intrigued he was and the more determined he became to bring her witness and the witness of many others to life and to the consciousness of the Oakhurst congregation. At the time of his initial discovery of Ida Wells, she had largely been lost in history, despite great and courageous work for justice and despite being a powerful force on the national scene from 1895–1920. Thanks to the efforts of many people, the history of her life is slowly being recovered.[3]

One of the things that impressed us about Ida Wells is that she was born in Marshall County, Mississippi, the same county in which all of Nibs's forebears were born. Indeed, the year of her birth (1863) was close to the year when Nibs's great-grandmother was born. In the oral history of Nibs's family, his mother knew his great-grandmother well and had told him many stories about her. Though his great-grandmother did not know Ida Wells, it is a powerful memory that they grew up and lived in the same era and in the same place, one a free white woman, one a black slave, both trying to find meaning in their lives out of poverty and out of the chaos that followed the end of the Civil War. Nibs's grandmother, known as "Big Momma" but officially named Willie Armour, had a family life remarkably similar to Ida Wells's. Big Momma's mother died when she was a young girl, and, at the tender age of eight, she began cooking for her family, standing on a wooden box to reach the stove. One of the standing jokes in the family that Big Momma used to say in her later years was "I do hope that when I die, St. Peter doesn't ask me to cook a meal in order to get into heaven. I don't know what my answer will be."

Ida Wells's parents both died in 1878 from the yellow fever epidemic, and Ida and six brothers and sisters were left to fend for themselves. The adult relatives of the Wells gathered to divide up the children among their families, but fifteen-year-old Ida stepped forward to insist that the siblings needed to stay together and that she would raise them. The relatives took it as a nice gesture but insisted that the children would have to be separated into different families. Ida Wells insisted right back that they would stay together under her leadership, and her argument and determination were so forceful that the adult relatives relented and allowed her to take charge.

She did take charge and began teaching in order to earn income, eventually moving to Memphis to earn a bigger salary. In 1884, on a train ride to Memphis, she refused to move out of the "whites only" car and was forcibly removed from the train. She sued the train company for discrimination and won. It was this fierce determination and vision of equality that gave her focus and purpose in a tidal wave of racism. She refused to accept the definition of racism that said she was inferior to white people. She lived her entire life under the definition that she was a daughter of God. In 1892, she saw the brutal face of white violence up close and personal. Her good friend Thomas Moss and two other black men were lynched in Memphis. The reason given for the execution by the white mob was that Moss and his friends had shot white people. The unspoken reason was that a white mob had attacked Moss's grocery store, and he had responded in self-defense.

The ideology of lynching for white people was that it was not a heinous act of racism but rather a necessary response to the bestiality and brutality of black people, often associated with the alleged sexual violation of white women. By this time, Ida Wells had started a small black newspaper in Memphis, and her journalistic skills were obvious. After her friend was executed, she was determined to show this death and other lynchings for what they were: executions of black men based on racism. She also began a meticulous study of all 615 other lynchings of the past two years in the United States, which showed that the vast majority had little to do with the alleged crimes of those who had been lynched. Instead, the lynchings were based in a huge crime that had been legalized: the power of white racism.

When her stories of the lynching of Tom Moss and others began to appear in her paper, the reaction of white Memphis was swift and violent. Her newspaper office was firebombed, and a bounty was put on her head. She was forced to flee for her life and finally ended up in Chicago, where she married Ferdinand Barnett and raised a family for the second time, all the while continuing her campaign against racism. She helped to found the NAACP, was a bridge between black women and the white women's movement, and continued to expose the racism permeating white America that sought to crush black people and other people of color. Throughout her entire life, she fought against the political and legal oppression of black people and against the internalized oppression that sought to make black people believe that they were inferior. Although she was not able to stem the tide of racism, her witness and her legacy serve as strong reminders of the continuing need to fight for justice and to proclaim the radical equality of the God we know in Jesus Christ: we are all claimed as daughters and sons of God, asked to live not in a hierarchy of domination but in a circle as members of the same family of God.[4]

These are the kinds of stories that we have shared in sermons in Black History Month, using people from the late 1700s up until the present day. We have sought to lift up those who have been witnesses for justice, whether they were Christian or not. We have searched for people who have refused to accept the definitions of racism, who have heard and who have believed a different voice, one telling them that all are children of God, rather than inferior black people and superior white people. Our purpose in these sermons is twofold. First, we want to lift up the necessity of hearing God's definition of ourselves and of others in the midst of the idolatrous definitions that permeate our hearts and our consciousnesses. As we noted in chapter 3, the struggle with racism is an entry point into the biblical realities and revelations regarding the powers that seek to define and take us over, all the while that God is seeking to redefine us and reclaim us as daughters and sons.

The second purpose of these sermons is to connect us all with the historical realities of the struggle for freedom, justice, and equality. While there has been and continues to be grave injustice in our midst, there is also a strong current of powerful witnesses who have spoken for and fought for justice and equality and dignity for all. Over the decades, their voices call out to us, inviting us to turn away from the idols and to hear a new definition of life, of ourselves, and of others. They ask us to join that great cloud of witnesses who seek to proclaim the new reality of the family of God, where there is no racism that proclaims that white people are superior; where women are seen as partners, not as objects and property; where the dignity of poor people is affirmed and where their needs are met; where our humanity rather than our sexuality is our central definition; and where all are welcomed to the table of God.

Our sermons in Black History Month have been an astounding success, not so much because of their outstanding quality (though we would like to think so), but because they touch a deep longing and a deep hunger in all of us. As we noted in earlier chapters, we have received many notes of gratitude for these sermons, and we have many names suggested to us by Oakhurst members for future sermons. In recent years, we have tried to include at least one white person in the series, sometimes as an example of white people's witness against racism, sometimes as an example of how racism captures the hearts of white people.

Our subjects over the years have included these folk: Sojourner Truth, Abraham Lincoln, Ellen and William Craft, Richard Allen, Frederick Douglass, Ella Baker, W. E. B. Dubois, St. Augustine, Robert Moses, William Trotter, David Walker, Myles Horton, Arthur Ashe, Bernice Reagon Johnson, Henry Highland Garnet, Barbara Johns, Thurgood Marshall, Paul Robeson, Barbara Jordan, William Lloyd Garrison, Howard Thurman, and Harriet Tubman.

Our series from 2001 can serve as an example. We began with William Still, a black man who was born in freedom in the North to a mother who had escaped from slavery but had been forced to leave some children behind. He became a leading conductor on the Underground Railroad in Philadelphia, connecting with a white man named Thomas Garrett in Wilmington, Delaware, to form a powerful team. William Still later wrote a book on the Underground Railroad in 1872, and it has become a primary source for the history of that movement.[5] Second in our series was the Rev. Francis Grimke, an African American who was actually born from the union of one of the richest white men in South Carolina, Henry Grimke, and his slave, Nancy Weston. Though Francis Grimke was emancipated at his father's death, he was later reenslaved by his uncle, who had been made his guardian in his father's will. He and his brother Archibald escaped from slavery, but he was recaptured and spent time in prison during the Civil War. After the war was over, he and his brother attended a freedom school in Charleston. Their intellectual skills impressed their teachers, and funds were raised to send them to Lincoln University in Pennsylvania. While there, they discovered their aunts Angelina and Sarah Grimke, white feminists and abolitionists and also sisters of Henry Grimke. The Grimke sisters supported them in their education, financing Archibald to be the first black graduate of Harvard Law School and sending Francis to Princeton Theological Seminary, where he was one of the first black graduates. From there, Francis Grimke would become pastor of Fifteenth Street Presbyterian Church in Washington, D.C., for almost fifty years and would become a strong advocate for racial justice and equality. He would marry Charlotte Forten, famous for her diary as a teacher at a freedom school during the Civil War off the coast of South Carolina known as the Port Royal Experiment.[6]

Third in our series was a sermon entitled "Thomas Jefferson, Sally Hemings, and Paul Coverdell," in which we emphasized the difficulty that "nice" white people like Jefferson and Paul Coverdell (former U.S. Senator from Georgia who died unexpectedly in the summer of 2000) have in escaping the power of racism. We have already reviewed Jefferson's struggles over race and equality in chapter 3, and in this sermon we discussed his relationship with his slave Sally Hemings and the DNA confirmation in 1998 that he had fathered at least one child by her.[7] Last in our 2001 Black History series was a portrait of Ella Sheppard, a young woman born into slavery who became a leader of the Fisk Jubilee Singers, the group of Fisk University students who introduced black spirituals to the white world. Sheppard's mother had almost drowned her when she was a little girl to spare her the horrors of slavery. An angel sent from God, an older black woman named Mamma Viney, intervened, however. These were the words that stopped Sheppard's mother from jumping into the Cumberland River in Nashville with her young daughter: "Don't you do it, honey. Don't you take that which you cannot give back. Look, honey, don't you see the clouds of the Lord as they pass by? The Lord has got need of this child."[8] The Fisk Jubilee Singers not only saved Fisk financially, but they transformed American music and influenced the development of jazz, the blues, gospel, and even rock and roll.

These sermons have brought a richness and a texture to our life together, emphasizing both the continuing power of racism and the witnesses who have fought against it and for a different vision of humanity. They have reminded all of us of the call to join in the river of witnesses for justice, whether or not the prospects for our efforts look promising or dismal. For all their power, the development of these sermons is not difficult. On almost every occasion, we have begun our research by consulting children's books from our local public libraries. These books give us an overall outline of the person's life and surrounding events, and from there we can dig into sources that cover the person or the issue more extensively. We encourage all those pastors in multi-cultural situations to use our approach or adopt it to fit their churches so that their congregations can begin to experience the richness and depth of these witnesses.

Women's History Month

March is Women's History month and includes the Sunday set aside by the PCUSA to celebrate Women's Gifts Sunday, based on the International Women's Day founded one hundred years ago on March 8. Each year we get a small team together to look over the material provided by our national office and then decide what we want to do for Women's Sunday. The service itself includes several women who are ordained and work in ministries with the homeless, the battered, and the forgotten, so the ideas gathered are strong and deeply felt. For our first service several years ago we chose the story of Esther. Since that same weekend our Jewish neighbors were celebrating Purim, the festival of Esther, we joined right in. The Sunday school classes studied the book of Esther. Each children's class was assigned projects, including decorating masks for the parade around the sanctuary. Many churches have such occasions, but they assign children to leadership roles at other times on Sunday morning, such as before church, or they only have such activities in the children's area during worship. Oakhurst involves children in our regular worship service because we see them as leaders now, not as leaders in-training for some future day.

Our Purim parade opened our hearts to hear anew the story of Vashti and Esther and their brave stand for their people. We invited women in our congregation who were "Esther" people to share stories about occasions when they had to be brave for others. Another year we took some of the feminine images of God and asked those who represented images such as Mother Hen, Mother Bear, and Mother Eagle to share in the message portion of the service. This past year our senior high girls planned and led our worship celebration as part of our denomination's emphasis on "The Year of the Child." They chose the seasons of life, and four women of the different stages of life spoke of their faith. We used the color yellow to represent youth, the color red to represent young adults, the color blue to represent seasoned adults, and the color purple to represent seniors. Our younger girls danced down the middle isle during the first hymn as the banners decorated with these colors were brought in. Later all attending worship were given small pieces of paper on which to write the names of women who are important in their lives, and these were taped onto these banners.

Humor and Humility

We are always learners. That is the key attitude to have in ministry within a multiethnic church. We are seekers and have come to rely fully on the Holy Spirit. Our personal prayer often includes beseeching God to let this worship, pageant, or program happen with meaning and with only a little confusion. We do not hesitate to say we make mistakes. Churches like Oakhurst cannot exist if everyone is afraid to make a mistake. We often remind our members and ourselves of this fact.

One story Caroline likes to tell on herself is a reminder of how humble we must be as we reach for new ways to tell the old story of seasons of celebrations. For several years we had many people who were from another country or who had traveled during the year to interesting countries such as India and Nicaragua. Caroline asked each of these people to work with a particular age group during November, and then to present a special tradition from that country during worship in Advent. Among our leaders we were blessed to have a young woman who was born in China and who, in fact, had been sent to the fields at a young age during the Cultural Revolution because her family was Christian. Caroline asked her what she would like to share with us from China during the Advent Season—she just looked at Caroline and said, "We have not been allowed to celebrate Christmas for seventy years. I do not know any Christmas traditions from China." After a great pause, we decided that we would learn a simple song from the new church of China and celebrate the New Year of the Rooster. We would use the color red, which in China is a symbol of good luck and, of course, a great Christmas color for everyone.

Just as humility is a must in multiethnic churches, humor is also important and must not be used to crush but to enlighten, especially the one who still has a lot to learn! Folks who visit with us say they never heard so much laughter in a church building. We enjoy each other very much because we believe deeply that God loves us in spite of ourselves, and because we are together in the wonderful work of redeeming love.

Dr. Charles Foster, in his book that included a study of our church, *We Are the Church Together*, sums up for us the joy of serving in a multiethnic church. He declares that "diverse people gather to wonder over the creativity of God's spirit in their midst." To choose the seasons of celebration can bring together the faith of a diverse group to explore all the ways that God continues to work in the life of the church and in the world in which we live today.

The best and most important way to begin is to check with your members. They are your best guide and greatest resource. Like a beautiful quilt, the many colors are added one at a time, and the small square that once fit on a lap becomes larger as stitches add the different colors.

Funerals

At our session retreat last year, our elders were asked to name some things they liked about Oakhurst. One elder replied, "This may sound weird, but I really like the way we do funerals at Oakhurst. I don't like the passing or the power of death, but I am moved by the celebration of life in our funerals. We really send our members home, and we celebrate their lives while we mourn their passing. It is a passionate affirmation of life, a worship that has been powerful for me."

We have already noted glimpses of our funerals in chapter 4, and now we want to look at them more thoroughly. From our emphasis on God's definition of us as daughters and sons in infant baptism to our claiming God's continuing promises to us through death, we celebrate the truth that we belong to God and that nothing will separate us from the love of God. We center on that journey and on that truth in our funerals. We encourage all of our members to have their funerals and those of their loved ones in our sanctuary in order to emphasize the connection with our community of faith and to emphasize that our space at Oakhurst has room to recognize the inevitability of death while also affirming God's power over death. We have a variety of music to soothe and to fire our spirits—from the plaintive and haunting sound of bagpipes playing "Amazing Grace" to African drums that help bring in the body and the family and that help send us out in recessional.

We ground our funerals in six principles: worshiping God, giving thanks for the life of the person who has passed, mourning our loss at his or her passing, claiming God's promises for the deceased and for ourselves, lifting up the particularities of the life of the one who has died, and sharing a meal together at the church after the body has been laid to rest. In these principles, we seek to emphasize that though death is frightening and painful, it is not the final word. The final word is God's promise of life and love and grace. We recognize that death threatens us and causes us anxiety most of our lives, but just as we emphasize God's definition and call while we are living, so we emphasize that same definition and calling as we pass through death. Our funerals at Oakhurst are thus an acknowledgment of the sting of death but also a celebration that death does not negate God's power and love.

Our first principle for funerals is that they are a worship service. We begin every funeral with these words: "We are here to worship God." That is the beginning and the end and the center. Death does not separate us from God's love, though it does cause us pain and anxiety. God's love is the ultimate and final word, and because of that, we gather at funerals to celebrate this great gift of God that sustains us even through death. Centering on God in funerals enables us to reaffirm the truth of the ancient church as well as the truth we experience daily: God is the center and the strength of our lives. We gather in community to worship God because we recognize that it is in community that God works to provide us what we need.

A second principle for our funerals is thanksgiving—giving thanks to God for the life of the one who has passed. In acknowledging the gifts we have received, we are not only speaking to God together, but also speaking to one another and praising God for the opportunity that we had to be loved and nurtured and challenged by the person whose passing we are also mourning. We give thanks for the engagement, for loving and being loved, and we affirm that this is at the heart of living, of life together. We tell stories about the person, and we acknowledge how much she or he meant to us. This process is easier when we are celebrating the life of an eighty-year-old person who has lived a full life. It gets more difficult when we are celebrating the life of a young father killed in a car wreck, leaving behind a wife and a two-year-old son. It is tougher when the person who has died of a rare blood disease is the single mother of a young son. Even in these instances, and especially in these instances, we give thanks to God for sharing the life and the gifts of the person who has died.

Our third principle acknowledges the power of death in our lives—we mourn the loss of the person who has died, whether ninety years old and ready to go or two years old with a whole life ahead. We do not emphasize death's claim. We emphasize instead that we are mortal creatures and that death is part of the process of living. The expression of this process of grief varies greatly from culture to culture. In many mainline white denominations, there is relative silence, with the family of the person who has died often secluded off from the rest of the congregation, as if to indicate that their grief must be private. One may hear a few whimpers, but often the unwritten rule is a stiff upper lip and few outward expressions of grief. The silence at times is deafening, as if to say that the hurt and the pain of the loss are so great and so powerful that they cannot be expressed and cannot be tolerated in public, in the community of faith.

In poorer white churches and in many black mainline denominations, there is a different expression of grief. Space is provided for its outward expression. Indeed, rather than being secluded, the family often processes into the congregation, getting one last look at the body in the coffin. Because everyone else in the congregation is seated, this expression of grief is very public, as if to say that expressions of loving, expressions of mourning, expressions of loss are expected to be part of life together in community. This ritual acknowledges the power of death and our mourning. It also acknowledges the power of God over death and affirms that God can receive and can handle our grief, our anger, our sense of loss, our hurt, and our pain. In some churches, the recognition of this necessity of public grief has led to the development of a group of women who will assist and comfort those who fall out in their grief, those who shriek and cry out. The "sisters" or "mothers" of the church are available to assist in public expression of grief before it takes over the worship service. In this way, the power of grieving is acknowledged but is not allowed to be overwhelming.

This ritual of the public expression of grief is a profound insight into the necessary component of community in both our living and our dying. It acknowledges how great a threat death is to us as individuals. It acknowledges how vulnerable each of us is, a biblical reality expressed by Isaiah 40:6–7:

> A voice says, "Cry out!"
>   And I said, "What shall I cry?"
> All people are grass,
>   their constancy is like the flower of the field.
> The grass withers, the flower fades,
>   when the breath of the Lord blows upon it;
>   Surely the people are grass.

Public expression of grief also acknowledges the cost of engaging and loving—sooner or later we will have to be separated from the ones we love, to say "good-bye" to one whom we have loved and who has loved us. It recognizes both the cost and the necessity of loving. The public expression of grief allows the individuals, the family, and the community all to acknowledge this complex but fundamental process of loving, engaging, and losing.

We affirm this ritual of grieving in our funerals at Oakhurst. The family of the one who has died processes in after everyone is seated and has a last look at the body. Public expressions of grief are allowed, and we have women (and men) ready to offer solace and comfort and guidance for those caught up in their grief. We recognize that death threatens us not only because we are losing a loved one but because death reminds us that we are not ultimately in control. We are mortal creatures, and nothing reminds us more starkly of that fact than a funeral. Death not only reminds us of one of the costs of loving; it also threatens the meaning of our existence—not only our own existence but the meaning of all that is. Does life have meaning? Do our lives have meaning? These questions confront us at funerals in ways that no other occasion allows.

We seek to acknowledge those questions and their threat to us at our funerals at Oakhurst. We acknowledge them in public because it helps to take away their sting by making them public in the community. We seek to answer them with our fourth principle: we claim God's promises for the one who has died, and we claim God's promises for ourselves. In the midst of our fears that we are not immortal, that we have no immortal soul that passes on to God when we die, we lift up the promises of God made to us in the life, death, and resurrection of Jesus Christ: death does not have the final word in our lives. God has the final word in our lives. No one put it more succinctly or more eloquently than Paul: "O death, where is your victory? O death, where is your sting?" (1 Cor. 15:55). We claim that just as we sought to trust God in life, we seek to trust God through death. In Jesus Christ, God promised us new life in this life and eternal life, and we claim those promises in our funerals. We claim those promises for the one who has died, and we claim them for ourselves.

We are rooted in Paul's powerful words in Rom. 8:37–39:

> No, in all these things we are more than conquerors through him who loved us. For I am convinced that neither death, nor life, nor angels, nor rulers, nor things present, nor things to come, nor powers, nor height, nor depth, nor anything else in all creation, will be able to separate us from the love of God in Christ Jesus our Lord.

We acknowledge how much the power of death dominates our lives and our consciousness, and nowhere is this felt more acutely than at funerals. We also claim the promises of God for all of us: death is not the final word; God is. What will our existence be after death? Will it be the twilight zone of Sheol seen in the Hebrew Scriptures? Or will it be the streets of gold of Rev. 21:21? We confess that we do not know, that the realm of the life after death belongs to God, not to us. Yet, we profess that God can be trusted, that the promises of God in Jesus Christ are true and steadfast. The comfort that we find in our funerals is not in our own power but in the power of God.

We acknowledge our vulnerability and our fear at funerals, and we lay claim to the promise that God is ready to meet those places of discomfort and anxiety and to overcome them. This is the "evangelistic" dimension of our worship service at funerals. We do not use funerals as a way to threaten those who are alienated from God. We use funerals to acknowledge how alienated all of us are from God, alienated as individuals, alienated as communities and institutions. We use funerals as we would any other worship service: as an opportunity for us to acknowledge that God is the center of our lives, our east and our west, our north and our south—and as an opportunity to acknowledge those places in our hearts and in our lives where we have denied that God is the center. We proclaim the stunning good news: in the midst of our alienation, in the midst of our rejection of God, God is claiming life and claiming us, promising us that the love and grace of God are the ultimate powers in our lives, urging us to say, "Yes."

The fifth principle in our funerals is what is often called the "eulogy," or the recognition of the life and the gifts of the one who has passed. It can include stories and testimonies by friends and family members, giving thanks for the life of the person who has died. It can include musical expressions of grief and affection and thanksgiving. All of our eulogies seek to center us in the knowledge that this person was a daughter or a son of God, someone whom God shared with us, someone from whom we were blessed to receive gifts from God. Nibs remembers a powerful testimony that helped him understand this dynamic. It came not in a funeral but in a hospital room where a man in his forties had just been declared dead from a rare blood disease, despite heroic, life-saving work. Some of his family were brought in the room, and Nibs was blessed to hear these words from the man's mother: "Son, I want to thank you and to thank God for all that you gave to me. You have been a light in my life, and I thank God for knowing you." As tears rolled down his cheeks, Nibs was struck by the power of a life and by the power of engagement, even at the very moment when the cost of that engagement was most clearly visible.

We root our eulogy in the words of the psalmist in Ps. 139:1–14: "[LORD], you examine me and know me, you know if I am standing or sitting, you read my thoughts from far away, whether I walk or lie down, you are watching, you know every detail of my conduct. . . ." (JB). In our eulogies, we acknowledge the gifts, the struggles, and the blessings of the lives of the people who have died. We do so not to say how great they were (or weren't) but rather to say how much we loved them and how much they loved us. We do so to acknowledge the importance of relationships and engagement and loving in our lives. We are aware that there are other traditions where such eulogies are not appropriate, where the name of the deceased is rarely mentioned, and where the emphasis is on the steadfastness of God. We recognize also that there is an equality in this approach—whether you were the most influential person in the community or the least, you will be treated the same in the funeral service. Yet our sense is that such an approach is not just impersonal; it is antipersonal. The attempt to provide equality in this approach diminishes the richness and the gifts of those who have engaged us. At the heart of our theology and our life together is this engagement, this willingness to cross over the boundaries of the world, and we want to acknowledge that in our worship at funerals.

We give thanks to God for the life of our loved one who has died. We acknowledge our grief and our loss, but we also proclaim God's healing and everlasting power in our lives—life now and life eternal. And, finally, in our sixth principle, we seek to demonstrate that God's power will continue in life and in our lives, even as we experience the powerful threat of death: we provide a meal for the family at the church after they return from the burial or at the conclusion of the funeral if the body has been cremated. In this way, we express in a concrete form one of the central ways that God's healing power works in our lives—the community surrounds us and undergirds us and shares in our grief and provides healing, helping us to experience that death is not the final word in our lives. The meal is an acknowledgement of the continuing impact of the community in dealing with the power of death.

In all of these six principles, we acknowledge the threatening power of death, but we also affirm the life-affirming and life-sustaining power of the God we know in Jesus Christ. By gathering as a community of faith in worship, we proclaim the necessity and the miracle of engagement and loving and caring for one another in the name of Jesus Christ. At our funerals, we seek to proclaim the inspiration of the words of Paul in Eph. 3:14–21:

> I kneel in prayer to the Father, from whom every family in heaven and on earth takes its name, that out of the treasures of his glory he may grant you strength and power through his Spirit in your inner being, that through faith Christ may dwell in your hearts in love. With deep roots and firm foundations, may you be strong to grasp, with all God's people, what is the breadth and length and height and depth of the love of Christ, and to know it, though it is beyond knowledge. So may you attain to fullness of being, the fullness of God himself.
>
> Now to him who is able to do immeasurably more than all we can ask or conceive, by the power which is at work among us, to him be glory in the church and in Christ Jesus from generation to generation evermore! Amen. (NEB)

Chapter Eight

Lord, I Want to Thank You:
Theological Principles

Time and energy: this is the heart of what I have learned at Oakhurst—time, energy, and work. The final irony of my story is this: My experience at Oakhurst—my ideal Church—has taught me a very un-idealistic nugget of truth. The ideal Church, when it answers its call, is not ideal because everyone shares my particular liberal polit-ical and social convictions. Rather, it is ideal—and indeed, this is the heart of its very survival—because regular people, of often varying political and social views, simply make commitments to each other and to the community—take the vows of baptism—and keep them. As Woody Allen might put it, it's all about showing up—and not just for Sunday morning worship—but for the real work of the Church, which is carried out by the many committees which need your participation. Oakhurst, God's right arm in the neighborhood, the city, and the world, needs you to show up, and to keep showing up—on Sunday morning, on Saturday morning work days, for week-night committee meetings, for choir practice, for tutoring and youth leadership . . . and the list goes on. If you want to be a part of Christ's presence in the world, city, and neighborhood, there's nothing fancy about it. It's just regular folk making commitments and keeping them. Join us. Just show up. It's hard work. But it's important work, and you'll be glad to be a part of it.

—Chris Boesel

*T*hroughout this book, theological principles have been emerging as we nar-rate the story of ministry in a changing context with all its promise and peril. In this chapter, we want to summarize those principles and offer them as guidelines for all of us engaged in this ministry, for all of us who want to do such engagement but are afraid, and for all of us who will be dragged into it through changing demographics or other influences.

The Importance of Presence

The first principle is what Chris Boesel addresses in the quote[1] that began this chapter: presence, or just "showing up," as he calls it. The importance of presence, of diverse peoples being in one another's spaces, of being in community together, cannot be overestimated. Presence is central. After all, the system of segregation was designed to separate diverse peoples, to prevent our being in one another's presence, to prevent the discovery of the humanity of the other, to prevent our discovery of the power of community. In this sense, being together, crossing the traditional boundaries of the world, is one of the most threatening and most revolutionary of any of our actions.

In our presence together as a diverse body, we affirm that God has broken down the dividing walls of hostility and intends for us to be a part of that work. In our presence together in diversity, we affirm Paul's words in Rom. 1:16: "For I am not ashamed of the gospel." In our presence together as a diverse body, we affirm that the power of God is greater than the power of race and racism and the other powers. We recognize the call to place ourselves in the presence of the other, despite how threatening such a call is to ourselves, to the other, and to the powers of the world. At its fundamental and most profound, the ministry of presence, of just showing up, is at the heart of our lives: worshiping together, eating together, playing together, working together, mourning together, calling one another into question and into a deeper place in ourselves, serving together, working for justice together, praying together. Here, in the ministry of presence, we find the presence and the power of God. On that level, it's simple—just show up. On that level, it's profound and complex—just showing up will call us into a whole new world.

An Attitude of Gratitude

"Lord, I want to thank you, for being so good to me." So sings our Sanctuary Mass Choir. It is a reminder of the attitude of gratitude that we ought to have. The problem is that real gratitude cannot be commanded. It must be called forth in response to our sense of having received a gift. In our life together, we seek to move all of us to the space in our hearts where we will discover God's gifts in our lives and will respond in gratitude. Our second principle centers on helping all of us understand that God's primary desire is not to make us good or perfect but to make us grateful, to make us loving. God wants our passion and not our perfection. Sharing our passion comes from the deep reservoirs of ourselves, places that cannot be commanded, places that speak out of our hungers and longings. As our second principle, we emphasize that

God has claimed us as God's children out of the depth of God's love for us. We are claimed as God's children not because of who we are or what we've done but because of who God is and what God has done. We emphasize this fact so that we can begin to feel and to experience God's gifts to us and to respond in gratitude.

This attitude of gratitude helps us to regain our primary definition of ourselves and of others: we are children of God; we belong to God. In a culture with such materialistic and technological power as ours, we often lose sight of the fact that we are creatures, that we are not authors of ourselves. In a culture rooted in racism and sexism, we often fail to see how much we are shaped and how much we seek to shape others by these demonic forces. The attitude of gratitude helps us to regain our center: we are children of God, and we belong to God. We can begin to hear God's voice calling us as God's children. We can begin to hear God's voice calling others as God's children. We can begin to understand the calling and the necessity of living together as sisters and brothers rather than as enemies or as those who fear monsters behind the walls.

In Jesus Christ, God has broken down the dividing wall of hostility and allowed us to see that those we thought were our enemies are rather our long-lost loved ones for whom our hearts have been searching. In this sense, God's sharing of diversity with us is a powerful gift. It causes us to reconsider ourselves and others—to reconsider the categories of the world that we have been taught and that we have accepted. It causes us to go deeper into ourselves to find where there is entanglement in our identities with the powers of the world. It causes us to begin to see a whole new world "out there" and "in here," inside ourselves. It helps us to turn around and to discover the God movement in our lives and in the life of the world. It causes us to find discernment about the grace of God.

The Power of Fear

And, of course, diversity can cause us to flee in fear. As we have indicated earlier, most of us do not see diversity as a gift of God. At best, we begrudgingly see it as something we ought to accept, as something that we are compelled to encounter, sort of like a vaccination. Most of us, however, are afraid of diversity and see it as an encounter to avoid. Our third theological principle is thus the power of fear in our lives. We call it a theological principle rather than an anthropological issue because the very nature of the journey that God has given to us means that fear is a powerful force in our lives. As we indicated in chapter 2, the biblical witness is aware of how much the power of fear dominates us. "Don't be afraid" is a sentence that seems to permeate every page of Scripture. Because we are conscious of our separation from others but also aware of how much we depend on others, anxiety permeates our lives. Because we are mortals who long for immortality, fear of the power of death is often a constant companion. It is here, in these places of fear and anxiety, that the powers seek to move in and take over our hearts. The powers of the world come into our hearts to offer us deals about ways of coping with the anxiety, and often we accept those deals long before we are even aware of them because they are offered by those who love us and nurture us rather than by the evil monsters of the world.

God is aware of the power of fear in our lives, and fear of diversity is one of the primary powers. The biblical stories demonstrate again and again God's movement to help us overcome the fears of our lives. Moses is afraid to return to Egypt to seek freedom for his people. Esther is afraid to step forward to save her people. Isaiah is afraid to become a spokesperson for God. Jonah is afraid that God can and will spare the people of Nineveh. Samuel is afraid to anoint David. The priest Zechariah is afraid when the angel Gabriel appears to him, as is Mary, the teenager, when Gabriel appears to her. The shepherds are afraid; the disciples are afraid; the people are afraid. God is coming to us to calm our fears and to offer us new life in precisely those places where fear dominates us. We seek to be ever mindful that there will never be a time when we are completely free of fear.

One of the ways that we encounter our fears is through the discipline of prayer. We are known as a "praying" church. We open or close most of our gatherings—whether worship or suppers or committee meetings—with an opportunity for people to share concerns and joys for prayers. We have a prayer group of older women that meets weekly and has done so for over thirty years with the avowed purpose of lifting up those in need of prayer. We receive requests from all over the city because people know that we will lift them up in prayer. We are grateful to this group of women who so faithfully carry out this task. In prayer we open ourselves as individuals and as a community to God's Spirit. We seek to create space in our own hearts and in the hearts of others for God to move. There is nothing magical about prayer life. It is the development of the discipline of opening ourselves to God with all our hopes and dreams and longing and failures and resentments.

It is in prayer that we reveal our vulnerability and our fears. In chapter 4 we discussed our development of the ritual in worship in which people are encouraged to publicly share their concerns and their joys. In this ritual, we all can acknowledge how vulnerable we are and how afraid we are of being vulnerable—even more so, how afraid we are of acknowledging how afraid we are. Early in the development of this ritual, middle-class white people often lavished praise on the black people who shared. Part of the praise came as astonishment and part of it came as a voice of longing to be able to do the same. Gradually, the while folks and everyone else began to share as it became clearer to us how much we fled from the idea that we were vulnerable. In our prayer life, we acknowledge the deep struggles that are in all of our hearts, struggles over life and death, struggles that are near the surface for some of us. For others of us, the struggles are buried deep in our consciousness because even to acknowledge them produces great anxiety. Whether we share in this ritual or not, we are all touched by this process, and we remember Paul's words in Rom. 8:26—"Likewise the Spirit helps us in our weakness; for we do not know how to pray as we ought, but that very Spirit intercedes with sighs too deep for words." In our prayer life together at Oakhurst, we acknowledge how afraid we are and how much we resist the gift of diversity. In our prayer life together, we pray for the Spirit to move us into the attitude of gratitude.

Say, "Yes!" or Engagement

The Gospel of Mark has Jesus beginning his ministry with the words "'The time is fulfilled, and the kingdom of God has come near; repent, and believe in the good news!'" (1:15). Our fourth principle acknowledges how much God wants us to say, "Yes." In the midst of all our struggles, in the midst of our fears, God asks us to say, "Yes," to turn around and see that whole new world, the new reality that God is bringing to fruition in Jesus Christ. Whether we have left for the far country as had the younger son in Luke 15 or whether we are grumpy about generosity as was the elder son in the same story, God is pursuing us. Whether we seem to have no idea who Jesus is, like the Samaritan woman at the well in John 4, or whether we are so captured by death that we can't even recognize the risen Jesus when he stands in front of us, like Mary Magdalene in John 20, God is engaging us and calling our names to help us to say, "Yes."

This movement by God underscores the importance of "presence," of being in the midst of the other, especially the diverse other whom we have been taught to fear and to perceive as our enemy. As vital and as necessary as "presence" is, it is not sufficient to enable us to say, "Yes." After we have allowed ourselves to stay in the presence of diversity, or after we have been forced into the presence of diversity, we must take the next step. We must cross boundaries and engage the other, and this engagement is our fourth principle. Just as God has engaged us in Jesus Christ, so we must engage one another in the name of Jesus Christ. Engaging one another and crossing boundaries are scary prospects. Initially, we will want to flee from such involvement, but just as God engages us, so we must engage one another. We will find cultural assumptions in our own selves, and we will find different patterns of naming, of foods, of celebrating, of mourning, of loving—all kinds of differences as we cross cultural lines and racial demarcations. In these kinds of encounters, we are asked to listen for the movement of God's Spirit rather than seek to prove that our way is superior.

In these encounters, we will find misunderstandings, distrust, and continuing barriers. The walls that have been built over several generations in our hearts will not be dissolved quickly. Racist assumptions will be revealed, and their depth and continuing power will shake us. In these encounters, we should remember that few of us have much practice at such engagement. The power of the system of race has kept us segregated from one another, and most of us believe in its power. As we encounter painful and difficult moments in our involvement with one another, we are asked to recall that most of us have no experience or practice in such engagements. Most of us have avoided the presence of diversity for most of our lives, and we are not accustomed to negotiating or exploring new territory with those we have counted as enemy. It is in these encounters, however, that we have the opportunity to discover both how narrow our focus has been and how great the possibilities are. We will find that we are much deeper and broader than we had previously imagined. We will discover that the other has rich stories and a rich tradition. We will learn that even though the cultural patterns are different, on a fundamental level, the issues are remarkably similar. We all want to love and be loved. We all want to know and be known, but life is so complex and full of struggles that we often lose our way as we seek to find love and revelation.

In our engagement, we are asked to listen and to share. The system of race has divided us so much that it is difficult to listen, and it is difficult to share. Our usual approach in such engagement is either overt attacks or covert manipulation that seeks to overcome the other and thus to disengage. Engagement of this sort is more akin to a battle where the object is not mutual assistance but defeat of the opponent. In this new approach, we are asked to see the other not as opponent but as potential partner who can help us to discover and to appreciate the depth and height and breadth and width of the love and power of God. The gift of diversity is that it can help us appreciate the majesty of God and the wonder of creation by revealing to us that we have made God too small and creation too narrow. The only way to appropriate this gift is through engagement with the diverse other whom we have been taught to fear but who may be, in fact, God's gift of revelation to us.

We have known the perils and the promise of the engagement of diversity at Oakhurst. We have wrestled and clashed and negotiated over differing worship styles, over differing approaches to financial stewardship, and over differing understandings of proper manners. We have engaged one another in primary issues such as the importance of people versus the importance of property, the nuclear family versus the extended family, and the acknowledgment of the body versus the life of the mind. We have *stunned* one another, and we have *stung* one another. For some, such engagement and such negotiation are too difficult, and they have left Oakhurst. Such departures are always sad, but we have sought to hold the line that such engagement and negotiation is fundamental if we are to step further into the God movement and receive the gifts of God. Those of us who stay do so because we make great discoveries about ourselves and about others and about God. Such presence—and the engagement that must grow out of this presence—provides us a glimpse of that new reality which God is bringing into the world in Jesus Christ.

The Necessity of Community

We live in the midst of a culture that is increasingly individualistic. This individualism is in itself a major barrier to engagement, but it must be confronted if we are to find redemption. That leads us to our fifth theological principle: the necessity of community. In our journey together at Oakhurst, we not only face the unusual barriers of race and class and gender and sexual orientation. We also face the fundamental force that all of us face in this culture: the power of individualism to disintegrate communities. For several decades, observers of American culture have been noting its growing power.[2] For our purposes, the idea of individualism centers on the belief that the individual person is the ultimate—and sometimes the *only*—reality. This idea of the power and importance of the individual is one of the gifts of Western, "white" culture to the world. It is also one of the great burdens.

This idea was rooted in the European Enlightenment as Europe began to emerge from the institutions of medieval times. Its power was so great that individual consciousness became the final arbiter of reality, and philosophers like Kant and Hume fretted about the consequences of such a movement. At the heart of this idea of individualism is the belief that the individual is of great worth and is the most important reality. It has been a welcome and necessary balance to the stifling power of communities and institutions that sought conformity and blind allegiance, that stifled creativity and the soaring of the human spirit. It has been the force behind human rights movements around the world, and its power continues to confront governments all over the world. In this sense, it has been a great gift.

Combined with materialism and technological power, however, individualism now threatens to disintegrate the many necessary communities that sustain our lives. In our North American culture, we have come close to perfecting the power of the individual, and now we are exporting that power around the world. Our culture emphasizes that the most important goal of our lives is to become independent, self-sufficient, and in control. The reality of our lives is that none of that is possible, and thus we are caught in a powerful dilemma of *wanting* to be a powerful individual while *needing* to be in community. The result is lonely, driven, and hostile people, longing to be loved and engaged but unable to even admit that we need such loving and engagement. The consequences of this struggle can be dire and frightening.[3]

At Oakhurst, we seek to lift up the power and necessity of community as a balance to the rampant power of individualism. We are assisted in this effort by deep tradition of the importance of the extended family. For African Americans whose "nuclear" families were often shattered by slavery, the extended family and community were necessary for the survival of individuals. That legacy continues today as a value that can counter the power of individualism. For Southerners, both black and white, the power of community and family is deeply rooted in our cultural memories. We know that we did not come into this world as self-sufficient beings. Someone had to feed us and love us and change our diapers and teach us how to walk and talk. We would not have survived as infants if someone had not taken care of us. And, if we live long enough, someone will have to take care of us at the end of our lives.

Our Reformed tradition also emphasizes this necessity of community. In both of our sacraments of baptism and the Lord's Supper, the power and the necessity of the community are affirmed. There are no sacraments in private. In the sacrament of baptism, we affirm the individual and his or her family, but we also stress the importance of the gathered community when the congregation vows to help nurture the person who is being baptized. In the Reformed tradition we baptize infants as a further guard against individualism and we deemphasize "believers' baptism" because we stress that God's love and grace are filling our lives and our hearts long before we know anything about it. How do we discover this love and grace? We discover them through the community who nurtures us and loves us and shapes us. In the sacrament of the Lord's Supper, we emphasize the community and its importance. Indeed, another name for the sacrament is "communion," indicating not only our connection with God but with one another. At Oakhurst, when the elders distribute the elements of the Lord's Supper to the people, we hold the elements until all are served, then take them together as a sign of the importance of community.

In our life together at Oakhurst, we give thanks for the dignity that each of us has as an individual. It is a dignity given to us by God's grace, by the fact that God calls us as a daughter or a son. This dignity cannot be taken from us by categories of the world that tell us we are better or worse because of our racial classification or our gender or our economic class or our sexual orientation or our nationality. It is a dignity rooted in the fact that we are children of God. We affirm the power and the dignity of the individual. We affirm the call of God to individuals to be witnesses and to make a difference.

We also acknowledge at Oakhurst the dangers of individualism and affirm that God has created us for community, that we belong to God and to one another. We affirm the gifts and the necessity of community. The difficult truth is that none of us would survive without community. It is a "difficult" truth because it emerges in the hostile atmosphere of individualism, where the ideas of meritocracy and works-righteousness dominate our culture. In this atmosphere, the gifts of community thus become liabilities and weakness. If we need someone, there is something wrong with us. In a strange twist of the imagination, the very gifts of community, provided to us by God, have become liabilities in our culture. No wonder our communities are collapsing!

The power of community also acts as a balance to the dangers of individualism. The community calls us out of ourselves to encounter the other, to hear the stories of others, to see how important but how limited our own view of reality is. The community offers us the opportunity to deepen and to broaden our understanding of ourselves, of others, of God, and of the world around us. Jesus summed up the entire law and prophets of Judaism into two principles: Love God and love neighbor. In so doing, he emphasized the tendency for us to remake God in our image rather than having ourselves remade in God's image. We often convince ourselves that we have put God at the center of our lives by reshaping God to conform to that center. Jesus counters this tendency by tying love of God and love of neighbor together. If we really want to know whether we have God at the center of our lives, we should check our relation to our neighbor. In that examination, we will gain discernment concerning where the center of our lives is located. And if we're wondering just who our neighbor is, Jesus gives us some strong clues in his story of the "Good Samaritan" in the tenth chapter of Luke.

Spirituality and Justice Together

Our life together at Oakhurst emphasizes both the gifts and the necessity of community. We affirm the dignity of the individual, but we also affirm the gift of community. We are given dignity as individuals by God's grace, but we experience that dignity only as we relate to others in community, in acknowledging and in celebrating that we belong to God and to one another. We acknowledge the gifts of both the individual and the community, and we seek to hold these in tension and in balance with one another. This tension leads us to our sixth theological principle at Oakhurst: the necessity of weaving spirituality and justice together. These two are often split asunder in American religious culture, but they must be interconnected if we are to live as the people of God. At the heart of the Christian faith is a belief that God knows us and desires us. Because of that powerful love in our lives, we have the promise that our lives—and indeed, all of life—have meaning. Because of God's claim in and on our lives, we have the assurance that no matter what the world tells us or does to us, we are the children whom God has claimed in Jesus Christ. We make the stunning claim that God knows us better than we know ourselves. At its most profound level, this grace is the gift of spirituality. It is the work of spiritual exercises to help us discover this source of love and grace and power in our lives.

In like manner, at the heart of spirituality is the understanding that God wills this same grace for all people. One of the great mysteries of our lives is that out of six billion people on earth and out of billions of other creatures in the universe, God knows our names as individuals. In the same way, God knows the names of the other individuals also, and God's work in this world is to establish a community and harmony of people who are created and claimed by God. The vocation of our lives is to acknowledge our Creator and to acknowledge our kinship to all the other creatures in God's creation.

As we have already noted, however, Christians in America have been adept at tearing apart the interconnectedness between "individual" and "community." White, southern Christians, for example, sought to understand our lives as children of God, and such an endeavor went well as long as we left it in the realm of the individual, as long as we emphasized that God cares only for individuals and individual salvation. If we took spirituality outside the church walls or outside individual consciousness, we ran squarely into slavery and segregation. These unjust institutions required white southern Christians to examine the terrible evil inherent in their very existence. The doctrine of spirituality required white Christians to confront slavery and segregation, but we could not do this because we gained so many benefits from them. In this manner, white southern Christians allowed our spirituality to be captured by slavery and segregation, and thus, we entered the time of "the racial captivity of the church." In chapter 1, we saw that this time was dubbed the "spirituality of the church," and it enabled white Christians to continue emphasizing God's grace in our individual lives while denying God's interest in or even God's power in communal lives and in institutions.

This story is repeated again and again in different contexts in American religious history, with the result that spirituality and justice are often pitted against each other. The modern phrase for this tension is "evangelism versus social justice," but at its roots it is the same issue that continues to plague us. Can we emphasize how important it is to accept Jesus Christ as our Lord and Savior while at the same time emphasizing how important it is to work for justice in seeking to join God in building the beloved community?

While there are notable exceptions—the Catholic Worker Movement, the Anabaptist tradition, and the Society of Friends, to name a few—for the vast majority of American Christians, this separation seems biblical and God-willed. But the separation of spirituality from justice has had disastrous consequences for American Christianity.

This separation has enabled people to believe that they are leading godly lives while exterminating native peoples, using slaves to work the land, and worshiping the money and capital produced from such a process. This separation has made a mockery of the biblical faith and has often been revealed for what it is: an attempt to reap the material rewards of injustice while congratulating ourselves for living lives worthy of our callings.

The difficulty with which southern white churches came into the civil rights movement reveals the depth of the power of this separation between spirituality and justice. Yet it is not confined to the South. Its power echoes in the memories of Wounded Knee and the Japanese internment camps; in the fields where migrant workers pick produce for us all; in the chicken-processing plants all over the country; in our prisons and jails, which often seem to serve as public housing for the poor, especially Hispanic and black people; in the streets of our cities and towns where homeless people huddle for warmth and safety; in the sweatshops in this country and around the world that produce the capital and the affluence that we believe is at the heart of life; and in countless other places where women and children and men are used by Christians to produce the wealth that we believe God wants us to have. In these and other instances, the witness of American Christianity is a clanging cymbal and a noisy gong, a sham for which Jesus Christ is deeply ashamed and saddened.

The only way we can accomplish this separation of spirituality and justice without being total hypocrites or deeply evil is to believe that it is the way God intends life to be, to believe that God is only interested in individual salvation. It is to accept the slaveholders' interpretation of Christianity. The sting of this separation has begun to be felt in the halls of American Christianity, and for the most part, our reaction has been to seek to overcome it through works of charity. We feed the hungry, clothe the naked, visit in prisons, provide housing for homeless people, and provide a few medical clinics for those who are "underserved." Although works of charity are a necessary step toward bridging the chasm that currently exists between spirituality and justice, in many cases we maintain the chasm by confusing charity with justice. Many contend that because feeding the hungry is a work of justice, the chasm has been bridged. Yet we fail to ask why, in a hugely affluent country like the United States, it is our public policy to have hungry people. As we noted in chapter 5, asking public policy questions is essential if we are to discover or recover our own individual spirituality. If we do not ask questions about justice, then we cheapen our own spirituality and settle for a diluted spiritual sense that is often little more than an echo of our complicity with the principalities and powers, much like southern white slaveholders did with Christianity and slavery.

In a way that sounds frightening to Christian ears attuned to the chasm between spirituality and justice, the only way we can hear our own authentic voice of spirituality is to ask questions of justice to ourselves and to our communities. There are, of course, many steps that we can take to begin to bridge this gap, but we must not allow ourselves to shrink back from the prophetic words of Amos:

> I hate, I despise your festivals,
>   and I take no delight in your solemn assemblies.
> Even though you offer me your burnt offerings and grain offerings,
>   I will not accept them;
> and the offerings of well-being of your fatted animals
>   I will not look upon.
> Take away from me the noise of your songs;
>   I will not listen to the melody of your harps.
> But let justice roll down like waters,
>   and righteousness like an ever-flowing stream.
>
> (Amos 5:21–24)

Only in this manner can we rediscover our own spirituality, and our restless hearts can begin to get a glimpse of home, as the African theologian St. Augustine noted so long ago: "Almighty God, you have made us for Yourself, and our hearts are restless till they find their rest in You."[4]

Let us again summarize the six theological principles that undergird and guide our lives at Oakhurst. Although there are many others, we suggest that these six are the core principles for guiding life in multicultural ministry or in ministry in any changing context:

1. The necessity of presence—God's presence with us and our presence with one another.

Chapter Nine

The Journey Is Our Home

My motivation for finding a church was my children. It was important to me that they had the opportunity to learn and know about God and Christianity, to give them a basis from which to examine and discover their own faith. In this area, Oakhurst has been all I could have hoped for. My children have been welcomed with open arms, and their heritage celebrated. They have an ongoing opportunity to see that people from different races and backgrounds can live and worship together, and even have fun in the process!

While I was delighted to find Oakhurst for our family, and enjoyed attending, I didn't think that I "needed" a church. I was doing o.k., had a decent sense of my spirituality, and was functioning well in the world. How we do fool ourselves! Oakhurst has been an incredible journey for me. The deep, beautiful faith of so many of its members has helped me feel stronger and more confident in my own. The portrayal of God's embracing love, regardless of how we struggle, has allowed me to accept myself in all my weakness, while working to move forward. Oakhurst has given me a better context for the work I do, and helped me share a message of hope and strength with the children we serve, rather than anger and self-pity. And as Nibs reminds us often in his sermons, it isn't always easy. The message I hear is sometimes challenging, disturbing, and counter to what I believe. Yet I am grateful for the opportunity it provides to shake me out of my complacency, reexamine my beliefs, and find new insight.

Oakhurst Presbyterian Church had added a richness to my life that I didn't realize was missing. I urge each of you to think about what Oakhurst has brought to your home and heart, and find a way to say thank you for that gift.

—Nancy Friauf

*T*hese words were written by one of our elders[1] who is the director of a shelter for abused and displaced children. She has seen, and continues to see on a daily basis, the destructive consequences of our culture's lack of appreciation of children. She sees the power of evil face-to-face in a way that many of us encounter only on the evening news or in the newspaper. She has brought a richness of experiences and a push for justice that has been a great gift to us at Oakhurst. She also brings a hunger for meaning and for community, and we seek to feed that with the bread of life at Oakhurst. She is like many of our members who work in public service and in justice ministries. In our daily work, we are confronted with the continuing power of evil and injustice, and Oakhurst is a place where we can find rest and renewal as we prepare to keep on being witnesses for our crucified and risen Lord.

The journey is our home.[2] The biblical witness is full of stories and metaphors that emphasize this theme. Abraham and Sarah are asked to leave their homeland to go on a journey to a new land. The biblical story of Israel is that of a journey—Jacob steals from his brother and lies to his daddy and flees for his life. Jacob and his family later travel to Egypt and end up in slavery there. Under Moses, the liberation begins but the israelites must also go through a long journey in the wilderness. Exile later becomes the occasion for the written transmission of the biblical witness. The followers of Jesus go with him on a journey, from Galilee to various places, then to Jerusalem. In his closing instructions, Jesus tells his disciples that they will be on a journey, going in ever-widening circles as they proclaim the new reality of the God movement. It is no accident that the first name of the people of Jesus is people of the Way. As followers of Jesus Christ, the journey is our home.

We seek to acknowledge this truth in our life together at Oakhurst. We recognize that once we set out on the journey with Jesus, it will take us into places in ourselves and out in the world that we thought we never could or would go. We recognize the amount of resistance that we have to this journey, and we recognize that we did not want to begin it at all. The movement of the city brought new people into the neighborhood and into the church, but many of the white people already there were not certain that these new people were really people, or they feared that their quality of life would change. Some of the white people who stayed felt that the proper course was to bring the new people in and assimilate them into white ways of life. They were shocked to learn that these "new" people brought gifts of their own. The dividing walls had begun to crumble, and brothers and sisters were found on each side.

Once the dividing walls began to crumble, we in the church saw an ever-widening circle for evangelism and for building the community of faith. Although the racial categories of black and white have been and remain primary, we have been called to consider other kinds of diversity: a growing garden of multicultural folk, women as partners with men, comfortable people and poor people, people with doctorate degrees with people who can barely read, people whose sexual orientations are different, refugees from Africa with African Americans—on some days, the list seems endless.

We are still negotiating much of this diversity, just as the early church continued to negotiate its many kinds of diversity. For us, it is not a source of despair, though it does depress us in times of conflict and struggle. Rather, it is a source of joy and deepening faith as we discover how rich and varied is God's multicultural garden, as we discover how much wider and deeper and broader God is, much more so than we thought when we were confined to a monocultural view of God. We have discovered—and continue to discover in new ways—how great God is. We have learned that God cannot and will not be confined to our categories, that God calls us on a journey in which we will discover ourselves and will discover others in ways that are both frightening and exhilarating.

In this book, we have attempted to narrate some of this journey, recognizing both its uniqueness and its universality. In some ways, we would hope that we are done, that we have reached the Promised Land. But we are aware of the biblical truth: the Promised Land served Israel much better as a vision than a present reality. Exile became a central theme for Israel, and the early church used it also. In many ways, we are all strangers and sojourners, trying to find our home. So we must stay with this truth, as difficult as it is at times: the journey is our home, a journey down into ourselves as individuals and as a community of faith, and a journey out into the world as we seek to be witnesses for the crucified and risen Christ.

Because of this metaphor of the journey, we are aware of the need for hospitality and welcoming to the table. The biblical witness tells us that because we are on a journey with God, hospitality is central; thus the Hebrew Scriptures emphasize hospitality often. It is why one of the central acts of Christianity is a community gathered around a supper table. Once we began this journey at Oakhurst, we found that we simply do not know who God will be bringing to our doors. We have had such a variety that it is difficult to name them all: black people, African people, comfortable people, poor people, white people, people addicted to drugs and alcohol, people who are convicted felons, homeless people, powerful people, Hispanic people, Asian people, gay and lesbian people, people hearing voices, people with doctorate degrees, bipolar people, activist people, middle-class people, Jamaican people, people who are seminary students, people who are heterosexual—the list goes on and on. Because of the nature of the journey, we adopted a stance of welcoming and hospitality. In 1990, our policy became this: We will welcome everyone that God sends to our doors.

We try to affirm the unique gifts of each individual and culture who comes to us, while at the same time trying to mold us all into one community of faith where respect for each other is deep and expectations of each other are high. We have read and studied the letters of Paul, which are sacred texts for this kind of journey, and we continue to try to live out his powerful words in 2 Cor. 5:16: "From now on, therefore, we regard no one from a human point of view." We believe that, like Paul in that same text, we have been given the ministry of reconciliation, by which we do not mean actions that encourage people who were previously alienated to be nice to each other, to smooth over the differences. Rather, our ministry of reconciliation entails actions and work that acknowledge the differences, take responsibility for the brokenness, and acknowledge accountability for the brokenness. In other words, it is a continuing journey in which we seek to welcome one another without denying the reasons we have not welcomed one another in the past.

Clarence Jordan, cofounder of the Koinonia community in south Georgia in 1942, put this vision in these terms:

"I will shed my spirit on all mankind." A spirit of partnership. The rich man will sit down at the same table with a poor man and learn how good cornbread and collard greens are, and the poor man will find out what a T-bone steak tastes like. Neither will shiver in a drafty house, nor have to move his furniture when it rains. Both will rejoice in the robust health of their children, who are not listless from having too little nor bored from having too much. They will discover the blessedness of sharing, the warmth of compassion, the quiet strength of humility, and the glow of gentleness, the cleanness of honesty, the peace of justice, the ecstasy of love. God's spirit will let a white man look into the eyes of a black man and see his soul; it will let a black man look into the eyes of a white man and see his soul. And they'll both know it's the soul of a man."[3]

In this kind of journey we can celebrate the gifts of our particular heritage and history but also learn their limitations. In this kind of journey we will learn how much we need each other, how much we need the insights of other people and other cultures in order to find our way home. In this kind of journey we can begin to celebrate the gifts of diversity and begin to give thanks and to trust in God.

And it is in this kind of journey that we resonate with the African American spiritual from which the title of this book comes: "Oh, Lord, hold our hands, while we run this race. Oh, Lord, guide our feet, while we run this race.

Oh, Lord, stand by us, while we run this race. Oh, Lord, we're Your child, while we run this race . . . for we don't want to run this race in vain."[4] On this kind of journey, we are aware of the difficulties. We know that the Israelites wanted to go back to Egypt after their deliverance from slavery: "'If only we had died by the hand of the LORD in Egypt, when we sat by the fleshpots and ate our fill of bread; for you have brought us out into this wilderness to kill this whole assembly with hunger'" (Exod. 16:3). As the old saying indicates, it is often easier to get the person out of Egypt than it is to get Egypt out of the person. Thus in this kind of journey we discover our fears and our captivity to the powers, and in this kind of journey we must continue to sing and pray, "Oh, Lord, hold our hands."

We have some awareness of the difficulties and fears that continue to confront us at Oakhurst. One of the scarier parts of this kind of journey is that we are also aware that we do not and cannot know all the fears and difficulties that we will face. We can only hope that our spirits have been deepened and broadened sufficiently to trust God when those unknown fears and difficulties appear in our midst. We must continue to sing, "Oh, Lord, hold our hands." We are aware, however, of some of those fears and difficulties now. As we mentioned in chapter 5, we are nervous about the numbers of white people moving into the neighborhood. We have affirmed that we are aware of the movement of the city, but we would rather it be in other neighborhoods! We discussed the liabilities of this movement for us in chapter 5, but we have also found that some of the white people moving into the neighborhood bring great gifts and a great hunger for God. They also bring a desire for diversity and see it as a gift rather than a liability. Our struggle lies in the sheer number of white people coming to us, for they threaten to disrupt the delicate balance of the ratio of black people to white people. The irony is that for most Presbyterian congregations, a growing number of white people moving into the neighborhood and coming to worship would be a blessing. For us, it is both blessing and potential curse, and some of the white people coming to us are aware of this ambivalence. When we have gone to visit them to talk about Oakhurst and about their interest in Oakhurst, some have indicated, "Are you sure you want more white people in the church?" Our answer is that we want more people in the church, but we are aware of the dynamics of such movement, and we appreciate the question.

This movement of white people into the neighborhood comes at a time when many black people and others classified as "nonwhite" have a growing sense that white people are incorrigible. Some are giving up on them, coming to believe that while there are a few white people who can be redeemed, most white people are beyond salvation. They have noted that forty years after the civil rights movement, the only progress that has been made has come at great cost, and much of that small progress is now being turned back. In this sense, there is less motivation now among black people to seek a place like Oakhurst than there was ten years ago. Are white people really worth such an investment of sharing intimate space in worship? For many young black and Hispanic people, the answer is increasingly "No."

To try to counter this trend, we are looking at ways to increase the number of black visitors in worship and the number of black people who become members. We are seeking funding for another part-time black pastor who will help us work in this area. We are trying to expand our community ministry beyond our immediate neighborhood, and we are seeking to develop a metro-wide strategy for maintaining our diversity. In all of these efforts and more, we are aware that our calling remains to welcome whomever God sends us, and we are aware that we won't always be able to control who these people will be or even be aware of who they will be. We are learning, and even beginning to celebrate, that the journey is our home.

The tension over welcoming gay and lesbian persons continues in our congregation and in our denomination. As we write this book, our denomination is in turmoil about this issue and may even split over it. We have found that many of the cultures we encounter at Oakhurst are even more conservative on this issue than white culture, but we have staked out our position because we believe that God is calling us to widen our tents and open our tables. In our journey together, we have found that it is much more than a "white" issue, as it was originally perceived at Oakhurst. Though our first openly gay folk were white, we have found that it is an issue that permeates every culture, and though it is not as broad or as deep as racism and sexism, it is nevertheless painful and unjust. In trying to come to terms with this issue, we have found that the ministry of presence is essential. Being together, supporting one another, struggling with one another, enjoying one another—these ministries of presence tend to take the edge off the issue and begin to open up arteries in our imaginations to receive the humanity of those we have previously tended to dismiss.

In this area, our practice of diversity is an asset. Though we do not claim that the oppression of gay and lesbian persons is the same as the oppression of African Americans, those who have been labeled as inferior or "nonwhite" have a basic foundation of knowing the necessity of welcoming those seen as "outcasts." The idea of welcoming, of hospitality, grows out of a long history of seeing and experiencing "Whites Only." It is this tradition, this legacy of suffering and exclusion and of liberation, this legacy of the journey, that we

believe will enable us to find a way in the wilderness to negotiate our differences and to welcome one another as sisters and brothers.

One final fear and difficulty is worth mentioning at this point, and it is a
difficulty that all churches face, whether they are multicultural or monocultural. That difficulty is the growing power of materialism in our culture and
in our churches, the idea that money is life, and life is money. It is a scourge
that has been part of our national identity for a long while, a shaping force in
our national character.[5] Ever since the Reagan Revolution of the 1980s, however, it has grown exponentially, and the long expansion of the stock market
in the 1990s only buttressed its claim to validity. Most Americans, and most
of our church members, believe that economic forces are ultimate and, that
money is the final arbiter of life. Such a belief shapes our theology and our
church life, and often our life of faith is an amendment to this juggernaut in
our society rather than the other way around. Because of the acceptance of
this belief, many of us and many of our churches are driven by the winds of
materialism and its expanding demands on our lives. The issues of family, justice, equality, and human dignity are required to stand in line behind the pow-
erhouse of materialism, and at best are required to eat only the crumbs from
its table.

We have seen our neighborhood shredded by this power of materialism as
white people fled because they were told that their property values would
plummet because black people were moving in. We have seen black people
forced out of the neighborhood by rapidly escalating property taxes resulting
from speculators raising the prices of houses because white people were moving back in. In our discussions with members, neighbors, and politicians
about this power, it was clear that most of us believe that market forces cannot be regulated in any way—God must take a back seat to market forces.

Our churches have developed few theological or communal models to
challenge this disease of "affluenza," as it was called by one of our members
in a sermon.[6] While we have spent countless hours and dollars and heartache
in our denominations over issues of sexuality, the real threat of materialism
has largely gone unchallenged. When challenges arise, they are usually dismissed as naïve and idealistic. Few of our churches will ever be threatened by
issues of sexuality, but all of us are under siege from materialism. The greatest danger of all, however, is that materialism has so captured our hearts and
our imaginations that we do not even know we are under siege by it. We only
know that we are stressed, lonely, disconnected, afraid, and hostile.

As we map out our journey at Oakhurst, these are some of the dangers that
we know we face in the days and years ahead. We are also aware that there
are other dangers that we do not yet see. In both these instances, we sing out

again, "Oh, Lord hold our hands." Yet, in the middle of these fears, we celebrate and praise God for the blessings that we have received on this journey. We have discovered deep reservoirs of faith and joy in ourselves and in others that we did not know existed. We have discovered that the diversity we feared (and continue to fear) is the very vessel that God is using to bless us. We have discovered a depth of humanity in ourselves and in others that we never dreamed was possible. In our daily experiences with one another, we have seen glimpses of the Promised Land, and at times we have known the joy and ecstasy of Mary Magdalene as she ran to tell the other disciples, "I have seen the Lord!" (John 20:18). We continue to be stunned by God as God takes us into places that we had thought we never could or would go. In some of these instances, we often shout out as did Peter, "Go away from me, Lord, for I am a sinful man" (Luke 5:8). More often than not, we find our hungers fed and our thirsts quenched in unbelievable ways, and we long for more of this living water, as did the Samaritan woman in her encounter with Jesus at Jacob's well (John 4:1–42).

This has been our experience in our journey together at Oakhurst, and we anticipate that it will continue to be our experience. We invite all of you to consider this kind of journey and to join us in it. Some of you are already in it and have much to teach the rest of us. Some of you are confronted by the possibility of this journey and are wondering whether to start out on it, with both fear and anticipation gripping your heart. Some of you are oblivious to this kind of journey and even resistant to it, but God will not leave you alone. God will be calling us all into this journey. Wherever you find yourselves on this spectrum, we hope that we have shared the deep joy and deepening faith that awaits you. There are struggles, to be sure, but we echo the words of Paul in Phil. 3:7–16, words that begin with these sentences: "Yet whatever gains I had, these I have come to regard as loss because of Christ. More than that, I regard everything as loss because of the surpassing value of knowing Christ Jesus my Lord."

In our journey together at Oakhurst, we have come to know Jesus Christ in a way that we were not previously aware was possible. As one of our elders put it recently, "Oh, I so much need to be at Oakhurst every week. It is the power that renews me and enables me to go out into the world each day of the week."[7] The power of which she speaks is not Oakhurst but what it represents for all of us: the diverse, gathered people of God, molded into a community of faith by the power of God's Spirit through our crucified and risen Lord Jesus Christ. It is a power that comforts us and confronts us and uplifts us and challenges us and gives us hope and vision and courage. A power that gathers us up and then sends us down into ourselves and out into the world to experience and to proclaim God's calling us children, God's calling to us to help provide space "where justice rules with mercy and love is law's demand."[8]

It is into this kind of journey that God is calling all of us. As you contemplate your own steps on this journey, our best advice and our best road map is our mission statement, which we adopted in 1990 and revised in 1998. We offer it as our conclusion:

> Oakhurst Presbyterian Church is a community of diversities. We come from different places, from different economic levels, from different countries of the world. We are a church in the city. Our life has known the movement of the city: we were once all of one kind. Then our church became multiracial and felt small and insignificant. And our people were afraid, afraid of ourselves from different races, and afraid of ourselves from different cultures. The faithfulness of those who stayed and those who came gave us courage. By God's power we have been given grace through what we thought was our weakness. In the midst of our fears God has surprised us and blessed us. The diversity, which we feared, has empowered us to confront God's truth in the world. In Jesus Christ the dividing walls of hostility have been broken down. Though we are born into diverse earthly families, our life together at Oakhurst has led us to affirm that we are called to be one family through the life, death and resurrection of Jesus Christ.
>
> Worldly differences fail to separate our folk. Instead, these differences are the threads that the love of Jesus Christ weaves into the one tapestry— Oakhurst Presbyterian Church. We are young woven with old, black with white, male with female, gay and lesbian with straight. We are employed woven with unemployed, poor with comfortable, strong with broken. We are courageous woven with disheartened, able with sick, hurt with healers. The world uses these categories to separate people from one another and to erect barriers between people. Our life together at Oakhurst Presbyterian Church, however, is a proclamation that people are more than just race, gender, economic class, and sexual orientation. We all find dignity at Oakhurst no matter the category in which society places us. And we celebrate that each difference finds its beauty and its strength in the Oakhurst tapestry.
>
> God is active in the life of Oakhurst and has given us a vision of hope. This vision has inspired our pastors and elders to lead us in the proclamation of the absolute power of God's love and God's grace. This vision is rooted in the truth that nothing in this world can separate us from the Love of God. Not powers, not principalities, not hate, not idols, not even death can separate us from the Love of God. And the very thing that we had feared—our differences—has empowered Oakhurst Presbyterian Church. Through God's grace what we once thought would destroy us has built us up. While alienation and separation persist in the city about us, the mission of Oakhurst Presbyterian Church proclaims that the Good News of the

Gospel breaks down the barriers of the world. In our coming together we become whole in Christ.

At Oakhurst the compelling sermons bring meaning to our stories and clarify the connectedness of our lives. The preaching sounds the Call to Justice. The Oakhurst message is not always a comfortable message. Rather, it is that we must seek to do God's will even when in conflict with the demands of the world. Our worship and work confirm that we are not impotent, that we are not just victims within this society, but through the Love of Christ we are empowered and are therefore responsible to act. We are The Good News realized. The work of our ministers guides our diverse peoples to weave the fabric that is our tapestry, Oakhurst Presbyterian Church.

FROM MANY THREADS, ONE TAPESTRY.
FROM MANY STREAMS, ONE RIVER.
FROM MANY BRANCHES, ONE TREE.
WE ARE OAKHURST.

Notes

INTRODUCTION

1. Jessica Page, "Community Interaction and Ritual Change: An Ethnography of a Racially-Mixed Church," unpublished paper, Spelman College, May, 2000.

2. "Black, White, and Angry," NBC Nightly News, (July 25, 1995); "Returning to Religion," All Things Considered, National Public Radio, Ted Clark reporting, (April 4, 1994); "Between Black and White," CNN Presents, Judy Woodruff reporting (December 3, 1995); "Practicing What You Preach," The Osgood File, CBS Radio (March 9, 1998); "Churches Still Struggling to Cross Racial Divide," Elizabeth L. Spaid, *Christian Science Monitor* (April 10, 1996): 3. "A Tale of Two Journeys," Nancy Ann Dawe, *Presbyterians Today* (January/February 1996): 21. "Who Me? Prejudiced?" John D. Filiatreau, *Presbyterians Today* (September, 2000): 12.

3. Charles R. Foster, *Embracing Diversity* (Bethesda, Maryland: Alban Institute, 1997). *We Are the Church Together*, Charles R. Foster and Theodore Brelsford, Trinity Press International (Valley Forge, Pa.: 1996).

4. For more information see Nibs Stroupe and Inez Fleming *While We Run This Race*, (Maryknoll, N. Y.: Orbis Books, 1995), esp. chap. 6.

5. Line from the hymn "Blessed Assurance," Fanny Crosby and Phoebe Palmer Knapp, *The Presbyterian Hymnal* (Louisville, Ky.: Westminster/John Knox Press, 1990), no. 341.

6. Verse from the hymn "In Christ There Is No East or West," *The Presbyterian Hymnal*, no. 439 and no. 440. In a revealing page in our denominational hymnal, there are two versions of music for this hymn. Hymn 439 is in the traditional tune of the European heritage; hymn 440 has the same words but with the traditional tune of the African American heritage. This page reminds us that different kinds of music come from different cultures. In our competitive society, people tend to see these two different tunes in opposition and seek to justify their own culture's music as superior to the other culture's music. One of the gifts that we have found in the Oakhurst experience is that these varieties in music are complementary rather than competitive. In another note of irony, the words in both hymns have also been changed to reflect more inclusive language from yet another cultural voice: that of the women's movement.

CHAPTER 1

1. Adopted 1989, revised 2000.

2. Those who feel that Race has lost its power should note that in the 2000 presidential election, the South went solidly Republican, consolidating a trend to tie race and the Democrats

together, a trend the Republican national party began after the Goldwater debacle of 1964. For more information, see Thomas Edsall, *Chain Reaction* (New York: W.W. Norton & Co., 1992) and Nibs Stroupe and Inez Fleming, *While We Run This Race* (Maryknoll, N. Y.: Orbis Books, 1995).

3. For a chronicle of the background and resistance, see Numan V. Bartley, *Rise of Massive Resistance* (Baton Rouge: Louisiana State University Press, 1969).

4. Stephen Lesher, *George Wallace: American Populist* (New York: Addison-Wesley, 1994), 174.

5. Manning Marable, "Facing the Demon Head On," *Southern Changes* 22, no. 3 (Fall, 2000): 4.

6. See chapter 3 for more discussion.

7. For an in-depth history of this decision, see Richard Kluger, *Simple Justice* (New York: Random House, 1975).

8. Joel L. Alvis Jr., *Religion and Race: Southern Presbyterians 1946–1983* (Tuscaloosa, Ala.: University of Alabama Press, 1994) 57.

9. Minutes of the Ninety-Fourth General Assembly of the Presbyterian Church in the United States, Part I, 1954, 193-95.

10. Donald W. Shriver Jr., ed., *The Unsilent South: Prophetic Preaching in Racial Crisis* (Richmond, Va.: John Knox Press, 1965), 15.

11. For more discussion, see H. Richard Niebuhr, *Christ and Culture* (New York: Harper & Row, 1951).

12. For a discussion of this doctrine, see Ernest Trice Thompson, *The Spirituality of the Church* (Richmond, Va.: John Knox Press, 1961).

13. Minutes of the Ninety-Eighth General Assembly of the Presbyterian Church in the United States, Part I, 1958, 37–39.

14. Minutes, 1958, 226–28.

15. Alvis, *Religion and Race*, 97.

16. Minutes, 1964, 154–55.

17. Shriver, *The Unsilent South*, 51.

18. Alvis, *Religion and Race*, 97.

19. Ibid., 102.

20. For a good discussion of these issues, see Clarence N. Stone, *Regime Politics: Governing Atlanta 1946–1988*, (Lawrence, Kans.: University of Kansas Press, 1989).

21. Ibid., 30.

22. Ibid., 68.

23. Minutes, Session of Oakhurst Presbyterian Church, Decatur, Georgia (November 12, 1963).

24. Minutes, Session (March 14, 1966).

25. Minutes, Session (July 5, 1964).

26. Merry Esther Porter, *When The Stranger Is Us: Identity and Vitality in the Racially Diverse Church*, (unpublished thesis; Atlanta: Candler School of Theology, Emory University, 1992), 106.

27. Minutes, Session (July 2, 1968).

28. For background on his work, see Alvis, *Religion and Race*.

29. Porter, *When The Stranger Is Us*, 117.

30. Charles R. Foster and Theodore Brelsford, *We Are The Church Together: Cultural Diversity in Congregational Life* (Valley Forge, Pa.: Trinity Press International, 1996), 69.

31. *Presbyterian Hymnal*, no. 354.

CHAPTER 2

1. "All Things Considered," National Public Radio (April 10, 1994).

2. Letter from Edwin Albright, Executive Presbyter, Presbytery of Greater Atlanta, to Nibs Stroupe, (November 30, 2000).

3. Sermon preached by Joan Salmon-Campbell at Oakhurst (September 17, 1989).

4. For the biblical bases of these powerful stories, see Matt. 14:22–33 and John 20:1–18.

5. W. H. Auden, "Song: Stop All the Clocks," in *Modern British Poetry*, ed. Louis Untermeyer (New York: Harcourt, Brace and World, 1958), 465.

6. The Larger Catechism, *The Book of Confessions PCUSA*, (Louisville, Ky.: Office of the General Assembly, 1996), 1.

7. Oakhurst Mission Statement

8. James M. Washington, ed., *A Testament of Hope: The Essential Writings of Martin Luther King, Jr.* (San Francisco: Harper and Row, 1986), 265–66.

9. Letty Russell, *The Future of Partnership* (Philadelphia: Westminster Press, 1979), 37.

10. Ibid., 56.

11. *We Are the Church Together* (Valley Forge, Pa.: Trinity Press International, 1996), 90.

12. We are aware that many scholars are skeptical about Paul's authorship of Ephesians, but these verses seem so attuned to his theology that we call them Paul's words.

13. See Wink's trilogy on the powers: *Naming the Powers, Unmasking the Powers, Engaging the Powers*, all published by Fortress Press, Minneapolis, Minnesota.

14. Wink, *Naming the Powers*, 104–05.

CHAPTER 3

1. Nibs Stroupe and Inez Fleming, *While We Run This Race* (Maryknoll, N. Y. : Orbis Books, 1995), 138–41.

2. Definition from Task Force to Combat Racism of the Presbytery of Greater Atlanta, 1999.

3. Jacques Barzun, *Race: A Study in Superstition* (New York: Harper and Row, 1965), 35.

4. George Orwell, *Animal Farm* (New York: Harcourt, Brace & World, 1954).

5. S. T. Joshi, ed., *Documents of American Prejudice*, (New York: Basic Books, 1999), 11.

6. Joshi, *Documents*, 272.

7. Ronald Takaki, *A Different Mirror: A History of Multi-Cultural America* (Boston: Little, Brown, & Co., 1993), 93–97.

8. For a fascinating discussion of the Thomas Jefferson/Sally Hemmings history, see *Jefferson's Children*, (New York: Random House, 2000) by Shannon Lanier and Jane Feldman.

9. For an illuminating history of the Irish and race in America, see Noel Ignatiev, *How the Irish Became White*, (New York: Routledge, 1995).

10. For more discussion, see Stroupe and Fleming, *While We Run This Race*; Thomas Gossett, *Race: The History of an Idea in America* (New York: Schocken Books, 1963); Theodore Allen, *The Invention of the White Race* (New York: Verso, 1994).

11. Thomas Edsall, *Chain Reaction* (New York: W. W. Norton, 1990), 182.

12. August Meier, *Negro Thought in America 1880–1915*, (Ann Arbor: University of Michigan Press, 1963), 190.

13. James Cone, *Martin and Malcolm and America* (Maryknoll, N. Y.: Orbis Books, 1991), 290–91.

14. Spencer Perkins and Chris Rice, *More Than Equals* (Downers Grove, Ill.: InterVarsity Press, 1993), 97.

15. Derrick Bell, *Faces at the Bottom of the Well: The Permanence of Racism* (New York: Basic Books, 1992).

16. Stroupe and Fleming, *While We Run This Race* 77–78.

17. Task Force to Combat Racism.

18. For a fuller discussion of these issues, see Stroupe and Fleming, *While We Run This Race*.

19. For a history of redlining, see Kenneth T. Jackson's *Crabgrass Frontier*, (New York: Oxford University Press, 1985), 197-218. For testimony on its current practices, see "Testimony of William J. Brennan, Jr. before the Committee on Banking and Financial Services, U.S. House of Representatives, May 24, 2000.

CHAPTER 4

1. Christopher John Farley and Sylvester Monroe, "The Gospel of Diversity," *Time Magazine* (April 24, 1995), 64.

2. *Meditations with Meister Eckhart*, Matthew Fox, editor, Bear and Company, Santa Fe, NM, 1983, p. 34.

3. Nibs Stroupe and Inez Fleming, *While We Run this Race* (Maryknoll, N. Y.: Orbis Books, 1995), 147–48.

4. Charles R. Foster and Theodore Brelsford, *We Are the Church Together: Cultural Diversity in Congregational Life* (Valley Forge, Pa.: Trinity Press International, 1996), 78-79.

5. Letter from Rebecca Linafelt to James Andrews (April 21, 1993).

6. Bernice Johnson Reagon, *We Who Believe in Freedom* (New York: Doubleday, 1993), 141.

7. Jessica Page, Community Interaction and Ritual Change: An Ethnography of a Racially-Mixed Church," unpublished paper, Spelman College, May, 2000, 9.

8. Ibid.

9. Farley and Monroe, "The Gospel of Diversity," 64.

10. Diana L. Hayes and Charles S. Ndege, *Were You There? Stations of the Cross* (Maryknoll, N. Y.: Orbis Books, 2000).

11. Foster and Brelsford, 84.

CHAPTER 5

1. Charles R. Foster and Theodore Brelsford, *We Are the Church Together: Cultural Diversity in Congregational Life* (Valley Forge, Pa.: Trinity Press International, 1996), 82.

2. Jessica Page, "Community Interaction and Ritual Change, 18. (see note 7, chap. 4).

3. Dom Helder Camara, Randy Schutt, Inciting Democracy, Spring Forward Press, Cleveland, OH, 2001, p. 41.

4. Robert Frost, "Mending Wall," in *Perrine's Sound and Sense: An Introduction to Poetry*, ed. Thomas R. Arp (New York: Harcourt Brace, 1997), 290.

5. Ernie Suggs, "No alternative: Everyone's moving—Upscale private homes to replace subsidized apartments in Lake Claire," *Atlanta Journal Constitution* (October 5, 2000): JB–13.

CHAPTER 6

1. Loretta Jefferson, "Congregational Study of Oakhurst Presbyterian Church," unpublished paper, Candler School of Theology (April, 1997), 12.

2. For more on this important phrase and its insight, see Henri Nouwen, *The Wounded Healer* (Garden City, N. Y.: Doubleday, 1972).

3. Nancy Friauf, "What Oakhurst Means to Me," *Oakhurst Log* (November, 1998): 9.

4. Letter from Bill Wyatt to Oakhurst Congregation (May 17, 1997).

5. "Blessed/Woe" Sermon by Edwin Searcy, University Hill Congregation, Ontario, British Columbia, Canada, (November 1, 1998): 2.

6. Letter from Toby Sanders to Nibs Stroupe (May 10, 2000).

7. Chris Boesel, "What Oakhurst Means to Me," *Oakhurst Log* (October, 1997): 5–6.

8. Christine Callier, "What Oakhurst Means to Me," *Oakhurst Log* (November, 1997): 4.

9. Christopher Farley and Sylvester Monroe, "The Gospel of Diversity," *Time Magazine* (April 24, 1995): 64.

10. Letter from Buddy Hughes to Caroline Leach and Nibs Stroupe (June 6, 1995).

11. Letter from Elizabeth Wilson to Nibs Stroupe (March 6, 1995).

12. John Turnbull, "What Oakhurst Means to Me," *Oakhurst Log* (October, 2000): 4–5.

13. Letter from Rebecca Linafelt to James Andrews (April 21, 1993).

14. Lorri Mills, "What Oakhurst Means to Me," *Oakhurst Log* (November, 2000): 4–5.

15. Letter from Mary Gould to Nibs Stroupe (December 18, 2000).

16. Sermon by Keisha Scales, Guilford College Worship, Greensboro, North Carolina, (March 18, 2001): 2.

17. Tanya Myers, "What Oakhurst Means to Me," *Oakhurst Log* (November, 1999): 7–8.

18. Stroupe and Fleming, *While We Run This Race* 170 (see note 1, chap. 3).

19. For more information about the impact of this migration, see Nicholas Lemann, *The Promised Land* (New York: Alfred A. Knopf, 1991).

CHAPTER 7

1. Charles R. Foster and Theodore Brelsford, *We Are the Church Together* (Valley Forge, Pa.: Trinity Press International, 1996), 77.

2. His initial encounter with Ida Wells was in *Black Foremothers*, by Dorothy Sterling (New York: Feminist Press at the City University of New York, 1988).

3. See, for example, *To Keep the Waters Troubled: The Life of Ida B. Wells*, by Linda O. McMurray (New York: Oxford University Press, 1998), and "Ida B. Wells," History on Video, Rex Barnett, Atlanta, Georgia, 1993.

4. For a powerful story of Ida Wells, see her autobiography, lovingly collected and preserved by her daughter: Alfreda M. Duster, ed., *Crusade for Justice*, (London: University of Chicago Press, 1970).

5. William Still, *The Underground Railroad* (1872; repr. Chicago: Johnson Publishing Company, 1972). See also Judith Bentley, *Dear Friend: Thomas Garrett and William Still* (New York: Cobblehill Books, 1997).

6. For more information, see Randall K. Burkett and Richard Newman, eds., *Black Apostles: Afro-American Clergy Confront the Twentieth Century*, (Boston: G. K. Hall, 1978; Darryl M. Trimview, *Voices of the Silenced*, (Cleveland: Pilgrim Press, 1993).

7. Shannon Lanier and Jane Feldman *Jefferson's Children* (New York: Random House, 2000).

8. Andrew Ward, *Dark Midnight When I Rise: The Story of the Jubilee Singers* (New York: Farrar, Straus & Giroux, 2000), 5.

CHAPTER 8

1. Chris Boesel, "What Oakhurst Means to Me," *Oakhurst Log* (November, 1997): 8
2. See Philip Slater, *The Pursuit of Loneliness* (Boston: Beacon Press, 1970); Robert Bellah, et al., *Habits of the Heart: Individualism and Commitment in American Life*, (Los Angeles: University of California Press, 1985); Robert D. Putnam, *Bowling Alone* (New York: Simon & Schuster, 2000).
3. See Octavia Butler, *Parable of the Sower* (New York: Warner Books, 1993); Gibson Stroupe, "Preaching on Covenant in an Age of Individualism," *Journal for Preachers* (Decatur, GA: Pentecost, 1992): 23–26.
4. Saint Augustine, *Confessions* (trans. Henry Chadwick; New York: Oxford University Press, 1991), 3

CHAPTER 9

1. Nancy Friauf, *Oakhurst Log*, (November, 1998): 5.
2. This is a line from one of our favorite songs, "Lead On, O Cloud of Yahweh," by Ruth Duck in *Everflowing Streams* (ed. Ruth C. Duck and Michael G. Bausch; New York: Pilgrim Press, 1981), no. 77.
3. Clarence Jordan, *The Substance of Faith* (ed. Dallas Lee; New York: A Koinonia Publication, Association Press, 1972), 159–60. We are aware of the exclusive nature of the use of the male language of "mankind" and "man" instead of "humanity" and "human," but we decided not to bracket it. It serves as an example that the journey is still our home.
4. "Guide My Feet," African-American spiritual, arranged by Wendell Whallum, *The Presbyterian Hymnal* (Louisville, Ky.: Westminster/John Knox Press, 1990), 354.
5. See, for example, the foundational study *People of Plenty* (Chicago: University of Chicago Press, 1954), by David M. Potter and a more recent volume by Juliet B. Schor, *The Overworked American*, (San Francisco: Harper Collins, 1991).
6. "Affluenza," sermon by Buddy Hughes at Oakhurst, August 16, 1998.
7. Conversation with Christine Callier.
8. Duck, "Lead On, O Cloud of Yahweh."